VILLARD  NEW YORK

Tales of the Failed, Dumped, and Canceled

Edited by Jon Friedman

Library of Congress Cataloging-in-Publication Data
Rejected : tales of the failed, dumped, and canceled / edited by Jon Friedman.
    p. cm.
  ISBN 978-0-345-50096-0 (pbk. : acid-free paper)
  1. Failure (Psychology)—Humor.   2. Literature rejected for publication.
3. Entertainers—United States—Biography.   I. Friedman, Jon.
   PN6231.F28T35 2009
791.092'2—dc22
    [B]   2008044686

Printed in the United States of America

www.villard.com

9 8 7 6 5 4 3 2 1

Book design by Liz Cosgrove

To my mom and dad—for laughing when Andy swung his spaghetti all over the place (and many other reasons).

I take rejection as someone blowing a bugle in my ear to wake me up and get me going, rather than retreat.

—Sylvester Stallone

Contents

Introduction

[Complete with my editor's notes]

Jon Friedman

Hi, Doug.

I had this idea to open the introduction of my book by specifically saying hi to anyone named Doug. **[I can't tell you how many introductions to books I have seen where the author begins by saying "I thought of starting the book this way . . ."]** The idea being that if your name actually is Doug, it would kind of blow your mind and you'd keep reading and then tell your friends what happened and then they'd run to the bookstore to see if the book was also specifically saying hi to them, but then it wouldn't; it would still be saying hi to Doug and then they'd be like, "It's not saying hi to you, Doug. It's some other Doug. It still says Doug." And then they'd put the book down. So I rejected the idea outright. Not to mention, so did my editors. This, of course, is why I then *did* open the book by saying hi to a Doug. **[So I think you should cut this entire section.]**

[This graph is boring and a little wooden] For nearly five years I've been hosting a live comedic variety show in New York City called "The Rejection Show," which features the rejected material from professional and up-and-coming comedians, writers, artists, cartoonists, filmmakers, musicians, actors, and any and all kinds of creative types who also have entertaining, interesting stories to tell about being turned down. "The Rejection Show" has had the actual writers from *Saturday Night Live* share sketches that never made it to air—sketches that were never seen because they were shot down during the show's official writers meeting or dress rehearsal. Writers from *The Onion* have presented headlines that never made it into print, and when they were read aloud, audiences reacted in a way that reading accepted funny news headlines would never have inspired. **[Clunkily worded]** Ordinary people stop by the show to read scathing breakup letters they received or love letters that they wrote to the guy or girl for whom they had an unrequited crush. Sometimes it's clear that the material is simply not funny enough, but mostly we're left wondering, "How could that have been rejected?"

[START INTRODUCTION HERE! A good intro always starts with a punchy first sentence] I never imagined I would end up doing this sort of thing. It's not exactly a childhood goal to strive toward working with unwanted material. But as my career in the entertainment industry progressed, it became clear that working with rejection just might be "my calling." During college I got an internship in the press and publicity department at NBC. My initial interview was on September 10, 2001, and I left knowing that I had gotten the position. And by "position" I mean showing up five days a week from 9 A.M.–6 P.M., spending all day, every day, clipping out articles from all the major publications that had any mention of any show or personality on NBC, and then making a packet out of those articles, photocopying those packets, and distributing them to the various offices at "30 Rock."

For no pay. The morning after my interview, the world fell down.

My time at NBC was an invaluable experience. I got to walk through the famed *SNL* and "Conan O'Brien" offices, dropping off those press packets to every desk. You'd be surprised how much you can learn just by walking around. I learned about the difficult pathways it takes to gain acceptance and saw what a long, hardworking, yet rewarding road it actually is **[this is cheesy sounding]**. There were specific ways of doing things and many unwritten rules of what *not to do*, especially as an intern. Of course my **[Jewish]** mother asked me, *"How come you didn't knock on Tina Fey's door and introduce yourself?"* or

"Why didn't you give your writing to Conan O'Brien?" but the thought of doing so didn't sit right with me. **[Too serious Jon. Lighten up.]**

On my last day at NBC I had my first real *completely self-induced* form of rejection. The previous night, I had printed out a bunch of my own *SNL*–style sketches and brought them in with me, though I wasn't quite sure what I would do with them. As I left the publicity offices to make my final handout run, I grabbed my sketch packet and went down to the 17th floor where the *SNL* offices are. (Studio 8H, where *SNL* is performed, is on the eighth floor.) I went into each small cubicle, putting the press clippings on each desk as I normally did. The closer I got to Tina Fey's office the more nervous I felt. I don't know why I thought she'd be in there; she never once was in her office when I came through. **[And if she was there, would I hand her my writing and explain that I, Jon Freidman, am the next . . . or look down at the floor like usual—you need some more description]** I didn't know what I was going to do—if I was going to give her my writing or not do anything at all. I turned and practically leaped into her office with a dopey, nervous smile, all ready to say "hi."

No one was there.

I moved toward her desk, put her press packet down, and dropped my own scripts directly into her garbage can. I didn't do it because I thought my writing wasn't good enough, or that someone like Tina Fey wouldn't care. I did it because I wanted to know that writing and art are worth more than just *hoping* someone else can "take a look at it." **[I THINK YOU GET YOUR POINT ACROSS WITHOUT ALL OF THIS]** So I turned around and walked out. [NB: This past year I submitted a writing packet and some of the exact scripts that I dropped in the garbage were included.]

After NBC, my career in rejection was molded and nurtured in different areas in my life. I went on to intern in the development department at Comedy Central where it was my job to go through the piles of unsolicited material and mail out the rejection letters. I did the same thing at the *New Yorker*, in their cartoon department. It was great to see what people were creating and sending in with the hopes that they'd be published or put on the air. A lot of it was terrible, some of it was great, but mostly all were entertaining because of the mindset in which I was viewing them. I knew that no matter what, pretty much the entire pile of work was going to be rejected. Knowing this, I was able to enjoy the material in a DIFFERENT way. It was simply more fun to view or read because a certain level of "judging" pressure was off. They'd already been judged for me, which, counterintuitively, allowed me to truly judge them for myself to find what I personally liked or didn't like within each one. Not to mention, it also made me feel better about my own work.

[Need stronger transition]

Then came a new kind of rejection that I had not yet experienced and it hurt more than any of the others combined.

I got dumped by a girl. **[A little too Dr. Phil]**

On the verge of despair, I eventually used my own disappointments as motivation to find the positive within the failures. **[A little clichéd]** And from that, "The Rejection Show" was born. From the start, I envisioned the rejected works as metaphors for "rejected" people. If these already-turned-down pieces can have new life entertaining audiences, then why can't we as people find new life in ourselves after dealing with hardships? Working with rejection was a way for me to find new life in both my work and myself by relating to others going through the same thing. We've all been rejected, disappointed, and heartbroken, and we've all felt worthless, low, and down because of it. That's why I believe so many people have connected to the idea. Comedy often masks something more serious that comedians want to express. "The Rejection Show" gives the artist a chance to share his or her ideas through humor, and the audience a forum to relate to the artist because of the universal nature of rejection. **[Again language is a little wooden, too formal, text book-y]**

It's been hugely rewarding to see artists discuss and display their "failed" work. "The Rejection Show" has given many entertainers a chance to dig out their old favorites (or unfavorites) that were once considered "not good enough" and get a new satisfaction from their own reject pile. It's a form of redemption—a way to move forward and find closure in something that may have caused pain in the past, have fun while doing it, and hopefully encourage others to want to do the same. **[Yes but you just said this]**

As for myself, I'm still a bit fearful of failure, but when it happens I know there can always be a way to use it to at least move toward success, and I owe that to the courageous collaborative efforts of the artists and audiences who have embraced their own failures on- and off-stage at "The Rejection Show." I've learned by watching and talking with these people to take risks instead of running away. It's all about laughing at our mistakes and missteps while still believing that what we have and who we are can always be useful, insightful, entertaining, funny, and valuable. **[Cheesy! Predictable!]**

Rejection can and should be your ally. No matter what kind of work or art you do, no one else can tell you that what you have is not good enough. Only you can say when you have failed. Each level of success opens up a whole new set of rejections and failures that we have to face. The cycle never ends, but we can find ways to adjust with each new experience. **[Too serious. Need to end with something light and funny.]**

I've seen you perform before, and while I've read about it, I've never seen *The Rejection Show*, alas. Double alas: I regret my schedule will not allow me to participate in the book. But thank you for thinking of me.

—John Hodgman, writer, actor

I'm so sorry—I thought I was going to be able to come up with something—but most of my "rejected" material is live and in person and I don't have recordings of the silence. Thanks so much for thinking of me and I can't wait to read it!

—Maria Bamford, comedian, actor

Thank you for the offer but I am pretty overwhelmed with my own projects right now. Sounds like a great idea. Good luck!

—Greg Fitzsimmons, comedian

My rejected story already appeared in the book *Fired*. Would that be a problem for Villard?

—Andy Borowitz, writer, comedian

It Takes a Village

Ophira Eisenberg

Like most things that go south, it all started with much promise. I was typing away on my computer, preparing a story for a reading show when I received a strange email:

> Subject line: the funniest girl in the world
>
> Hi Ophira,
>   I hope you don't mind me emailing you but I want to come to your upcoming show in Rhode Island, as you keep popping up in the funniest places over here and I keep laughing!
>   In the spirit of brilliant, hilarious women, take a look at this: (link to her blog)
>   Great to hear about all your amazing successes. Keep it up!
>   Best,
>   Sarah F.

I thought "Wow—that's really nice, thanks!" Which quickly turned to "what successes is she talking about?" I really didn't have much going on. No successes to speak of other than keeping seventy dollars in my bank account. But I wanted to know more about this mysterious fan and my unknown successes, so I clicked on the link that led me to Sarah's blog. The blog contained a story called "The Funniest Girl in the World." It read:

> "The story begins in the land of bagels and mussels and bowls of coffee and bags of cheap avocados and soul-searching university

students looking for love, or a reasonable facsimile thereof. This boy meets that girl through a mutual friend. This boy and that girl see a few movies together, take some long walks together, wear some weird masks together, and pretty soon, they are a *thing*."

The story names the players *that girl, this girl,* and *that boy.* As I read, I figure out that I am *that girl.* Sarah F is *this girl* and *that boy* is my ex-boyfriend Michael. I went out with Michael for eight months, T-WEL-VE years ago. We broke up rather unceremoniously over the phone. He was in Chattanooga visiting a sick aunt; I was in Montreal alternating between freaking out about finals and smoking pot. And that was it. For us. My life moved on and we didn't keep in touch. I had heard he got married, evidently to Sarah F. Who signs their name Sarah F? That is so fifth grade. Luckily, so am I . . . and I read on.

The blog continued on about how Michael once said *that girl,* or me, was *the funniest girl he had ever met.* This is big news to me. I don't remember *that guy* laughing at anything I ever said, let alone thinking I was the *funniest.* Plus he dumped me! What kind of guy dumps *the funniest girl he's ever met?!!*

This particular comment sends Sarah F off the deep end of insecurity, and the next thing she knows she's Googling me. Because that's what we do. . . . we Google the things we hate. I sent Sarah F a saccharine sweet email back and we exchanged a few more, but my show in Rhode Island ended up getting cancelled and slowly her fascination with me wore off. Or maybe the rough patch in her marriage ended.

I decided to switch gears and instead tell that story at the reading show. After all everyone loves adult women acting like jealous preteens. I was right because the next day I receive an email from an editor at *Marie Claire* magazine who was in the audience.

Subject: from *Marie Claire* editor

Hi, Ophira! I'm an editor at *Marie Claire* magazine, where we're always looking for new writers to pen laugh-inducing stories for us. I caught your show last night and thought you were great. If you would be interested in contributing to our magazine, which targets a largely urban, progressive, professional bunch of women 25–35, send us a few clips that would make us capital-L Laugh, and any story ideas that you may want to tackle.

Have a great weekend!

I had never read *Marie Claire* magazine. I stopped reading women's fashion magazines at a certain age because they made me feel poor, ugly, and un-tanned. However, I would *Love* to write for one and, more important, get paid glossy magazine dollars.

I send some pitches—girly things I assume the *Marie Claire* culture will like and receive an email back that they are looking for something specific.

Hi Ophira,

Do have you any interest in writing a "sex stunt" piece for us? I'm taking pitches from a few writers for our June issue. If you have any ideas (and are willing to open up to a million readers!) send them my way by Monday. Could be a new product, new sex mode/positions/etc., anything! Crazy—and of course, likely to be hilarious—is good!

In the past we've featured: a woman who used a make-a-dildo-of-your-boyfriend's-penis kit (I'm sure there's a better name for it); a woman who tried a bunch of kama sutra positions, a woman who went to an orgasm competition (she won), and a woman who wore a remote-control vibrator in her underwear for a day.

Cheers!

"We're really looking for something edgy," she explains to me on the phone, "the more provocative and edgy the better." What the hell does *Marie Claire* find edgy? A day without toner? Ignoring your horoscope? Whole milk in your coffee? Sex stunt? Will I ever write something I can send to my mom? After a great deal of thinking and brooding I send off a pitch knowing full well that it is so not *Marie Claire*.

WORKING TITLE "Confessions of a First-Time Dominatrix"

A hilarious first-person story of a comedian's foray into the world of S&M.

One fearless writer enters the underbelly of S&M to find out if the whips, chains, and riding crops of this dark world are terrifying, humiliating, or—worst of all—appealing.

Turns out the editors at *Marie Claire* love it! They want me to start on it immediately and give me a small budget of $300 for cabs, cover charges, and an outfit. As a first-time writer I'll have to write it on spec, meaning once they approve it they'll pay me, but no guarantees. Whatever! I'm excited and willing to prove myself. The only problem is—I don't want to explore the world of S&M. Isn't life hard enough as it is? But I can't really back out now. These are the kinds of situations I put myself in all the time. How bad could it be, right? Throw on some pleather, go to a party, and degrade some guy for kicks. No big deal.

So I did it. I explored, I went to a class, a dungeon, a newbie night, a party, and a club. And I wrote about it. By the end of the process, the article had been so carefully edited and *Marie Clairified*, I could hardly recognize my own voice.

As you can imagine, the article never made it to print. As it was being "sherpa-ed" (their word, not mine) to the higher-ups to be approved, my supportive and faithful editor quit to take a fancy job writing on the west coast, leaving me stranded. But it's not her fault. Supposedly, it's Ashlee Simpson's fault. As my article was floating around, Ashlee Simpson appeared on the front cover of *Marie Claire* with an accompanying article stating something to the effect of "I love my face and body and I would never change anything!" The only problem was, that very month she appeared on TV and in other publications with a brand-new face-altering nose.

This caused a lot of commotion at *Marie Claire*. People were fired and remaining editors were instructed to trash any pending articles they had on their desks, in fear that another embarrassing outdated fact would be printed, further mocking the magazine's credibility.

They needed to build back their readership, one "What Your Shoes Say About You" article at a time.

The following are some horrifying highlights from this piece that never saw the light of day, about a community of people who never see the light of day. It was all about my experiences in the New York S&M community, covered in a thick coat of sparkly pink nail polish.

> I've been a stand-up comic for eight years, so I'm no stranger to the sadomasochistic relationship. My audience laughs: pleasure. They don't laugh: pain. Not long ago, an attractive blonde and her heavily tattooed boyfriend approached me after seeing my act. "Come be a dominatrix at our S&M Club!" they said. "We think you'd be a natural!" Apparently I could earn upwards of $200 an hour to discipline men—no sex involved. Sounded like an average night at a bar, minus the paycheck! I politely declined, but their words stayed with me.

This is true. This strange couple suggested I audit a private S&M session to see what I thought. I was new to New York at the time, and broke, and they seemed perfectly nice and reasonable. I called my then boyfriend back in Toronto. He was unamused. "Really, you came to New York so you can take some sleazy job working in the sex industry? You are certainly living the dream!" We broke up a few months later, but his words stayed with me.

> I've never really been a "natural" at anything, with the exception of learning to eat exotic new foods. And when it comes to that, my motto is: "You don't know unless you try." With that in mind, I finally decided to check out the underground world of S&M.

That's a universal progression. First you like Thai food, next you like cock and ball torture.

> I call my friend David—cool, gay, and always up for an adventure—to accompany me. To the fetish club. The club is

located across the street from a church in an upscale neighborhood. I wonder if anyone has ever had to decide: fetish club or church. There's no sign, just a black metal door. We pull it open and descend down three long flights of stairs—giving me plenty of time to rethink my decision. But we keep going.

Isn't "cool, gay, and always up for an adventure" redundant? Couldn't we have just stuck with gay? The adventure wasn't that neat or planned, either. It was Saturday and a draft of the article was due on Monday. Although I had done a ton of research, I hadn't exactly dominated anyone. I was booked to do a stand-up set at 8 PM, so I figured I would go to the fetish club around 10 PM.

After the show, I decided to have a drink with the other comics at this divey gay bar. I ordered a double Grey Goose on the rocks. And then another. And then another. Then I made the mistake of admitting to a couple of people that I was planning on going to an S&M club and my outfit was in my bag. Of course they demanded I put it on.

I was plastered drunk, and it was like hitting a red carpet! Everyone was screaming and catcalling, cell-phone cameras were flashing, gay guys were touching me! Finally! My heels were about as high as my blood-alcohol level, and I couldn't manage either. I saw my friend David sipping a beer and looking very dapper in a pinstripe suit. I clumsily grabbed him by the tie and slurred, "Come with me to the sex club!" And he replied, "Um, okay." In the cab ride down, I threw up a little.

The S&M club isn't exactly what I expected. The "bar" doesn't serve alcohol, which is actually standard for S&M clubs— seems whiskey and whips just don't mix. And it wasn't . . . sexy. A matter of fact, there is no sex allowed. What happens between these walls is a lot more comparable to a scantily clad wrestling match than an intimate encounter. Some people choose to be topless, some even bottomless, and others in Planet Hollywood sweatshirts.

Think lots of Planet Hollywood sweatshirts and other people who you wish would put one on. It was the unsexiest place I had ever been in my life. And even though it was midnight on a Saturday night, the fetish club was . . . empty! There were seven people wandering around bored . . . in leashes.

The next thing I know, a shirtless man with a shaved head appears out of nowhere. He crawls toward us, stops at my feet, and then peers up at me demurely. "I am at your service, Mistress, if you so choose," he says in a hushed voice.

"Not now!" I reply in the most authoritative tone I can muster, trying to hide my shock. "Maybe later."

David and I decide to explore. In one room we find a wooden structure that looks like a giant asterisk, with straps at the end of each plank. I can't, for the life of me, picture myself strapped onto it. In another, a medieval metal cage awaits. It's connected to a hoist so that it can be raised to the ceiling. We encounter a wall dotted with various kinds of restraints and shackles, with a net thrown in for good measure. David begins to chant, "Cages and shackles and racks! Oh my!" But as a big fan of Renaissance Faires, he gets most excited when he sees the wooden stocks. He sticks his arms and feet through the appropriate holes, and says, "Okay, now spank me!" So that's what I do. I smack him with my bare hand, since I don't have anything else to use. A small crowd appears out of nowhere.

It's difficult to properly express in words alone just how excited David was by the stocks. We'd need a graphic novel for that . . .

The next thing I know, a very short, mustached guy wearing lots of black leather approaches. He opens a canvas doctor's bag and hands me a wooden ruler. "Try this," he advises.

"I'm just a novice," I tell him, in keeping with what I learned in class.

"That's why I gave you the ruler," he replies, smiling. "By the way, I'm Bill."

As I whack David's bum, Bill gives me gentle pointers: "Aim more for the bottom fleshy area. Now alternate hitting with rubbing in small circles. Good! Good! Try paddling around his inner thighs . . . look at that! You're a natural!"

That couple was right—this does come easy for me! I stop when I hear David, who's been smiling the whole time, utter our safe words ("grande soy chai latte").

Actually, what comes easiest to me is my desire to gain someone's approval, in this case my new teacher Bill's. I am so focused on being his star pupil, I didn't even realize that I was beating the shit out of David. Until I heard him scream "SOY CHAI LATTE!" No need for the "grande."

I'm in shock at what just went down, but I have no time to reflect because men are now lining up before me to be punished. The guy who approached me earlier on his knees asks for permission to kiss my feet before I spank him. Why not? He bows down and begins kissing my feet, though he licks my shoes way more than my toes.

The guy kissing my feet abruptly stands up, yanks down his pants far enough to expose his black boxer-briefs, and waits for me to begin. I test different leather and wooden paddles out on him, including a very stylish leather riding crop. It's going along swimmingly until I miss his butt completely and smack him in the side with the handle. "Ohmygod, I'm so sorry," I squeal, then blush like crazy. That's the last thing you want to hear from your dominatrix—even worse than hearing it from your dentist (but not as bad as your gynecologist). "Are you okay?"

Kill me.

"Yes, Mistress. Thank you, Mistress," he mumbles. I focus on giving him a series of precise, well-placed swats as an apology, but I couldn't tell if my paddling efforts were really doing it for this strange guy. Was he getting hot? I was, but only from the workout I was getting while wrapped in shiny vinyl. He continued to want more but didn't seem . . . aroused. Maybe I'm not very good? Maybe he's expecting more? Maybe it's more a sense of relief, like having an itch that gets scratched . . . really, really hard? But he was so respectful and thankful after the play something must have clicked, right? Why be insincere at 1 AM in the fetish club? Wait a second. Why am I insecure at 1 AM in the fetish club?

What really went through my mind was "I feel icky. Can I go home now?"

I'm a little disappointed. I was hoping that being a dominatrix would make me *feel* something truly special. I'm enjoying the power trip, and all the attention makes me feel totally sexy, but it hasn't unlocked some magical place in my soul that ordinary sex can never reach. Is that all there is to S&M? Am *I* the weird one now?

What I originally wrote was, "Is that all there is to S&M? And if that's all there is my friends, then let's keep dancing, let's break out the booze . . ." But I guess their demographic doesn't worship Peggy Lee like I do.

When I stroll through my door at 2 AM, my boyfriend springs up from the sofa. "You look amazing, baby. Tell me everything!"

"It was all right," I reply. "I whipped and paddled a few nice strangers in front of a crowd. Then I finished my soda and left. In other words, it was just another Saturday night."

"How about you show me what you've learned?"

I'm exhausted, but the glint in his eye is intriguing. I pull off my jacket and tell him to hang it in the closet. He does. And from there, we have one of our best—and most fun—

encounters ever. I realize that what was missing at the club was intimacy. Once I add that to the equation, playing with power dynamics proves utterly thrilling. Which isn't to discount the other benefit I've discovered: When I want my boyfriend to clean the apartment, I grit my teeth and squeeze into my bustier. Then I ask. Works every time.

This paragraph is one of the most embarrassing things I have ever written. For one, what was really missing at the club was fun, sexiness, and alcohol. Secondly, when I came home, my boyfriend was sleeping. I washed my face, stripped off the smelly costume, and then passed out beside him. I spent the next six months writing the article and going through rounds of edits, complaining, and waiting for a paycheck that never came. That's as close as we came to practicing S&M in our apartment. Oh . . . and nothing motivates my boyfriend to clean the apartment. Life in the *Marie Claire* universe is so much simpler.

Why, in the end, the article was not published will always be a mystery to me. Was it really the fault of new-nosed Ashlee Simpson? Or the editors at *Marie Claire*? The S&M community? My Toronto boyfriend? Sarah F? Or does it all trace back to Michael dumping me twelve years ago? Maybe I should blame myself. Whatever the case may be, it wasn't just one person. It takes a village to reject me.

Ophira Eisenberg is a 2007 MAC (Manhattan Association of Clubs and Cabarets) Award Finalist for Best Female Comic, and has appeared on Comedy Central, VH1, E! Channel, and the Discovery Channel. She performs regularly at renowned comedy clubs across the country and also tours with The Moth, a NYC storytelling phenomenon, and she is featured on The Moth's *2006 Audience Favorites* CD. She is also a regular contributor for *US Weekly*'s Fashion Police, Gawker.com, MSN.com. Her writing has also appeared on Mr. Beller's Neighborhood (Story of the Week) and in the new magazine *The Comedians*. She also writes, produces, and vblogs for Comedynet.com.

A Tale of Rejection from *The Daily Show* (and Its Fans)

Bob Wiltfong

> I was rejected by *The Daily Show* repeatedly—not only by the people who run the show but by its fan base.

I was first rejected by the show in April of 2000. At the time I was an up-and-coming improv comedian in New York City whose day job was as a TV reporter and anchor on Long Island. In an unsolicited cover letter to the show's producers, I wrote:

> My name is Bob Wiltfong and I'm a performer at [an] improvisational comedy theater in Chelsea. I'm also known as Bob Butler. Butler is the name I work under for my job as a reporter and weekend anchor at News 12 Long Island (Long Island's answer to New York 1).
>
> I'm writing to you because for years now I've felt like I was in the wrong end of the business. For eight years, I've worked full-time as a news reporter/anchor at different TV stations around the country. I've won several awards for my work (most recently, two New York Emmys). But it's in spoofing the news that I feel my true talent lies. And it's certainly where my passion is!
>
> I've enclosed a nine-and-a-half-minute videotape for you to view. The tape contains work that I've done on Long Island (both for air and off-air) that, I believe, showcases what I bring

to the table as a writer/performer. I would like you to consider me for a job (in any capacity) with *The Daily Show.*

I hope to hear from you soon. I've always felt called to work on something like *The Daily Show.* I hope you're the one who gives me the chance!

Sincerely,

Bob Wiltfong (a.k.a. Bob Butler)

My heart-felt plea was greeted with silence. Rejection number one.

Rejection number two came a couple of years later. By this time, I had established myself as a relatively competent improv comedian in New York. I was doing shows two to three nights every week in the city and rehearsing and writing on most others. Some commercial agents started to take notice of my work and referred me to an acting class that was run by a woman who just so happened to be casting the latest round of auditions for correspondents at *The Daily Show.* She invited me in.

When I arrived at the casting office, I saw that some of the best young comedians in New York were also waiting to go in and give it their best shot. Many of my counterparts in improv were there too—including the guy who went in right before me, Ed Helms.

Ed and I had known each other for years while making the rounds in the city comedy circuit and were friendly with one another. Ed, matter of fact, had taken my spot on an improv team called Toast after I left it. In talking about our preparation for that day's audition, Ed said to me, "This isn't fair. You're a ringer." I remember thinking in response, "You're right. I *am* a ringer for this job."

Jon Stewart and the people at Comedy Central, unfortunately, didn't agree. I didn't even get a callback.

Ironically, Ed—the *non*-ringer—booked the job along with another improv comedian counterpart of mine, Rob Corddry. I would watch as their stars—along with Stephen Colbert, Steve Carrell, and company—grew bigger playing fake TV reporters. Meanwhile I went back to being a real one. It sucked.

Then 9/11 happened. And I finally decided life is too short to do a job that you hate. So in March of 2002, I quit TV news to pursue a full-time career in comedy and acting. One of my immediate goals was to write a one-man show about my experiences in news and try to get some industry attention for it. I spent a year-and-a-half performing the show (in various forms) throughout the city, getting it tighter and tighter, better and better.

That eventually led to me being put on a double bill with Ed Helms and his sketch group. Ed, by now, was a pretty big celebrity in comedy circles, so our shows were getting a fair amount of attention. Unbeknownst to me, one night one of the producers from *The Daily Show* came to check out Ed's show—and caught mine too as a result. He evidently liked what he saw because I received a call the next day asking for a demo reel of my work.

On September 30, 2003, I went into *The Daily Show* studios to audition with Jon Stewart to be a correspondent on the show. Things went well. I was offered a job as a freelance correspondent. I accepted. We negotiated and signed a contract. And as of November 14, 2003, I was *finally* going to work at *The Daily Show*!

Then nothing happened.

For months.

With no explanation.

I started to wonder if I was getting pranked. I mean, they did hire me, right? We did sign a contract and everything. So why weren't they at least calling to explain what was going on? Little did I know this would be a recurring pattern of behavior with them.

Things got even more curious in February of 2004 when I was watching the show one night and saw a new correspondent appear on the show. Was I out before I was even in? My worst fears were confirmed when a letter arrived at my house informing me that:

Central Productions LLC is not exercising Option One or
Option Two for your services pursuant to Paragraph 6 of the
Agreement, dated as of November 14, 2003, between you and
Central Productions LLC for [*The Daily Show* with Jon Stewart.]

That meant I was fired. I was *fired*!? What just happened? I called
the executive producer I dealt with on the show and left a deflated
voice mail for him, apologizing for anything I might have done that
led to this. He then called me back and told me the letter I received
was actually a mistake and that they did, indeed, still want to use me
as a correspondent on the show. Rejection reversed!

In April—about five months *after* officially being hired by the
show—I made my first appearance as a correspondent. My debut
story, however, was greeted by a whole new round of rejection! This
time from the show's fans on Internet message boards.

On the site, www.televisionwithoutpity.com, the following posts
appeared:

PB4Uleavehome: I'm not feeling this new guy. He doesn't have the
certain [Stephen] Colbert it factor.

Bungalow Joy: I'm not feelin' him either . . . He sounds very open
mike stand-up as opposed to news reporter-ish.

Joanie42: I'm glad he didn't try to directly emulate the masters!

Fortunately, the powers-that-be at *The Daily Show* liked what I was
doing well enough to give me more assignments. Over the next year
or so, I regularly contributed new field pieces to the show and started
to build up a library of good work.

However, that didn't stop some of the show's fans from hating my
ass. Matter of fact, the Bob Wiltfong–bashing strengthened on
IMDB—which all of a sudden sprouted a message board devoted to
yours truly:

fyredriftwood (Tue Mar 29 2005): I've watched Bob's segments,
and I don't get what everyone else is seeing. Is he really that
funny? There's something off about him—he's sort of . . . CREEPY.

MercuryOne (Wed Mar 30 2005): I agree, he is very creepy. I think he doesn't really fit in with all the other more talented reporters on the show, he just doesn't seem to 'get it.'

fyredriftwood (Sun May 15 2005): He tries too hard. Don't like him.

SEOD_Rohan (Fri Jul 8 2005): . . . he tries too hard to be like Ed Helms.

fyredriftwood (Mon Jul 11 2005): And Ed Helms is the best on the show and we don't need another one of him. =)

TheLadyGreenleaf (Tue Nov 8 2005): "ps-bob sucks"

As I read these comments, I thought:

1. Who the *hell* is "fyredriftwood" and why does he hate me so much?
2. Where is the message board for me to rip *these* people a new one?
3. Why did they have to post this stuff on a permanent forum like the IMDB message board?
4. Who the *hell* is "fyredriftwood"!?
5. Am I really CREEPY?

The Daily Show saved up its biggest serving of rejection for me at the end of my stay there. They delivered it in the same way my first rejection from them was received: with silence.

In May of 2005, my contract came up for renewal. Without telling me, they started to audition new correspondents—including several friends of mine in improv. That, alone, didn't bother me. They had every right to hire (or fire) whoever they wanted to at the show. What did bother me was that they didn't pull me aside to explain to me what was going on—good or bad—and that I had to find out through my friends and coworkers awkwardly telling me about it. I figured that was a bad sign. I was a goner. Then . . .

The show offered to re-sign me for another year! Huh? We negotiated a slight raise for my work and I signed the new contract. It was a strange process but I was happy to be on board again!

Then nothing happened.

For months.

With no explanation.

The show never called me in to work again and, to this day, I still don't know what happened.

And I still don't know who the hell "fyredriftwood" is either.

Bob Wiltfong is a former correspondent on *The Daily Show with Jon Stewart*. Before pursuing comedy as a full-time career, he worked as a local TV news reporter and anchor, for which he won four regional Emmys and was nominated for fourteen others. His other credits include *Chappelle's Show*, *The Hoax* (starring Richard Gere), and *30 Rock*.

Blue Tongues

Mandy Stadtmiller

I wrote "Blue Tongues" and submitted it to National Public Radio's *This American Life* a few years ago. I never heard back from them, so this is how I knew it was rejected. I still love the story and I still love *This American Life*. It's funny; I met Ira Glass a few months ago, and I never even mentioned this story to him. Right now being a columnist for the *New York Post* takes up most of my creative time, which is a nice outlet for writing about my life. Really, in terms of rejection, I think the most important thing is just to keep doing it and keep getting better. I look back at this piece and I would have done it totally differently now. But I still love it. You just have to keep creating. That's the most important thing.

I am the daughter of idealists.

My parents resisted tradition in raising us. They resisted "having rules." They resisted "using labels." They resisted "wearing pants."

My sister Amie and I knew we were different, and we were okay with that. We were allowed to swear. We were allowed to criticize the establishment. We were allowed to call President Reagan a "little bitch."

Of course, my parents didn't abolish rules completely. We could not watch *Popeye*. We could not watch *Divorce Court*. We could not watch *Donahue* when the guest list was weak.

My mom was emphatic on a few points in particular. We could not pierce our ears. We could not say something "sucked." And most importantly, we could not eat sugar of any kind.

While other kids licked candy jewelry rings and bubble-gum cigarettes, we attended a regularly scheduled snack hour at our family's one-level house at the bottom of the hill on 60th Street. We ate okra and broccoli. We ate jicama and sprouts. We ate carrot sticks, celery stalks, carob chips, granola bars, applesauce, asparagus spears, tangerine wedges, banana sandwiches, ginger chews, dried pineapple, and trail mix.

We were the laughingstocks of the cul-de-sac.

When I was nine and Amie twelve, we decided to take matters into our own hands. It was Easter Sunday, and we were still reeling from a particularly good egg hunt in the backyard. Amie discovered Barbies near the lemon trees. I found Matchbox cars under the honeysuckle vines. We crossed the street to our neighbors, Kelly and Carrie, who were seven and eight, so we could gloat.

Our humbling came quick. Laid out across their glass coffee table was an obscene array of chocolate bunnies, chocolate chicks, chocolate cats, chocolate dogs, chocolate turtles, chocolate dinosaurs, and various chocolate creatures from the sea. I reached for a jelly bean. Amie nodded approvingly.

Questioning authority had never tasted so lightly tangy. I knew I was in trouble, but it wasn't until I went to the bathroom later and stuck out my stained black tongue in the mirror that I saw the full extent of the damage done. In desperation, I pumped soap from the hand dispenser and slathered the liquid on my tongue, working it into a bubbly foam. I cringed. I spit. I winced. I repeated.

I vowed to never eat sugar again.

Later that summer, my sister—bolder, wiser, and totally not afraid of the mean girl up the street who used a spaghetti strainer and Clorox to dye her hair—reminded me of the transgression. Amie said she wanted to "take a bike ride." "I feel like taking a bike ride," she said. "Do you know what I mean?"

She meant candy.

"Yeah, I want to go for a bike ride, too," I winked back. Fight the power. Smash the state.

We pedaled furiously up the street. Past the Frogen Yozurt, past the sketchy college apartments, past the giant blinking neon Indian twirling a baton on the closed-down drive-in movie theater. We kept riding until God's divine number appeared above our heads. We had reached the everyday place for people on the go. The leader in convenience retailing.

What happens at 7-Eleven stays at 7-Eleven, we assured each other.

There were rows upon rows of Sweet and Sour Pops, Milk Duds, Jolly Ranchers, Bazooka bubble gum, Tootsie Rolls, Kit Kats, Snickers, Skittles, Life Savers, Hot Tamales, Mike & Ikes, Reese's Pieces, Butterfingers, Gobstoppers, Candy Necklaces, Charleston Chews, Banana Runts, Candy Buttons, Atomic Fireballs, Twizzlers Pull-n-Peel Cherry candy, Chupa Chups lollipops, and Jelly Belly Jelly Beans.

We ate ourselves sick.

Thirteen dollars, forty-six cents, and two hours later, we walked our bikes home. "We were just riding around the neighborhood," Amie instructed. "We ran into some people. We ran into friends. We explored nature. We had fun. Whatever you do, go straight to the bathroom."

We stopped dead in our tracks at the front door. My mom stood on the porch, arms folded, eyes wide. Way too nice.

"Hi!" she said, sitting down and blocking our paths. "How did the big bike ride go?"

We looked down.

"Good," I said.

"Great," Amie said.

"Really? Well, what'd you do? Where'd you go? Tell me all about it."

"Not much," Amie said. "Not much to say."

"Did you go down the big hill?" my mom asked. "That hill is so scary!"

My sister was defiant. "Look, Mom, it was just a bike ride. Nothing special, okay?"

I looked up, taking my lead from Amie and agreed. "Yeah," I nodded. "Regular."

My mom looked at me and turned to ice. "Stick out your tongue, Mandy. You too, Amie."

We looked diseased. Blue tongues, purple teeth.

"Grounded," my mom hissed. "For the rest of the summer."

I retired to my room to spend the summer with my collection of collections (snow shakers, pennies, postcards, stickers, restaurant coasters, stuffed animals, hamster food, dirty underwear). Amie returned to her Billy Idol poster and the sealed *Seventeen* magazines that she was not allowed to read until she actually turned seventeen. Gift subscription.

I wrote letters to tell my friends the news.

"Dear Maureen, I'm sorry I can no longer play with you, but my mother has lost her trust in me. You're kind of a liar anyway. Have a good summer—Mandy."

My sister did what she does best in times like these. She strategized.

The next day, she came to see me. She stepped illegally onto the brown furry carpet in my room.

"I know how we're going to get out of this," she said. "We clean the whole house. The whole, entire thing. Everything."

Idealist parents are kind of messy.

"What do you say?" Amie said. She folded her arms like my mom. She scared me.

"Oh," I said. "Yeah, definitely."

We used the intercom system set up in our bedrooms to work out the rest of the details. We would wait until my parents had gone for the evening. We targeted critical areas of need. Somehow I ended up with the bathroom.

Later that day, when my parents left for the night, we dug into the cleaning supplies. We skipped the Formula 409 and went straight for the Scrubbing Bubbles. My sister demanded perfection. When she came in to check my progress in my parents' bathroom, she wasn't happy with me simply shining and buffing the counter. I had to use a toothpick to clean out every groove in the control dial to my father's Water Pic.

When my parents returned home that night, they were speechless. Stunned and speechless. My sister was emboldened. "Now," she said. "What do you think of us now?"

My mom regained her composure. "Interesting," she said. "I see you've been doing a little tidying up around the house."

Amie interrupted. "We worked the entire time you were gone. And we thought about what we did. And we talked about it, too."

I kept quiet. I didn't want to screw this up. Instead, I did what I found helpful in a lot of stressful situations when I was nine. A headstand in the corner.

Their negotiations began. "What would you think about a month for the grounding?"

My sister was unimpressed. "A month?" she asked. "I'm sorry, but maybe you haven't seen the bathroom?"

"A week," my mom countered.

"A day," my sister held firm.

"A really long weekend," my mom said.

"Done," Amie replied.

I exhaled and rolled out of my headstand. I thought about what we did. But I did not talk about it, too.

Mandy Stadtmiller is a staff entertainment writer and dating columnist (About Last Night) for the *New York Post*. She is also a stand-up comedian and in 2006 won first place in the New York Underground Comedy Festival's Funniest Reporter in New York Contest. She is a fan of people who do interesting things in life despite how scary life can be. Her website is mandystadtmiller.com.

Rejected Sketches from *The State*

David Wain with Michael Ian Black

About a decade ago, my college friends and I were lucky enough to have our own sketch comedy show on MTV, *The State*. Our process involved us all writing sketches all day, then pitching the sketches to each other every afternoon at 3 P.M. The best sketches were then submitted to the network, then from those that were approved, a smaller number were selected for shooting, and from that group, we'd pick the ones to include on the show. But each of us wrote many, many pieces that never even made it past the first round. These are a few of my favorites from that list. Who knows why the group didn't like these? Maybe because they're *too* funny. You decide.

Cheese Factory

A cheese factory.

All the workers are standing by their stations doing nothing. All the machinery is off.

The BOSS comes in and talks to the FOREMAN.

> **BOSS**
> What the hell's going on here, Kelman? We're expected to produce 10,000 pounds of cheese per day. You better have a damn good excuse as to why nothing's happening!

FOREMAN

We all arrived right on time as usual sir, it's just that . . . no one can seem to remember how to make cheese!

BOSS

What do you mean? We've been making cheese here every day for 25 years.

FOREMAN

I know, sir. We've just forgotten how it's done.

BOSS

Well, call the Cheese Institute and ask them to fax us a refresher kit.

FOREMAN

Yes sir.

Cut to OFFICE—CHEESE INSTITUTE: Phone rings. Mr. Kelly speaks into the air.

KELLY

Cheese Institute. This is Mr. Kelly, can I help you?

Phone rings again.

OFF-SCREEN VOICE

Mr. Kelly, in order to talk on the phone, you have to pick up the receiver.

KELLY

Yes of course! (speaks into air again) Cheese Institute. Can I help you?

Cut back to FACTORY.

BOSS

This is getting ridiculous. Did someone release forgetting gas into this factory?

FOREMAN

Not that I can remember, sir.

BOSS

What the hell are we gonna do????

A strange voice is heard off-camera.

MACGOOGLE

You're going to go out of business forever.

BOSS

Who's that?

We see MACGOOGLE, a weird-looking man in a rainbow-colored suit and sunglasses and a cane and a strange voice.

MACGOOGLE

Allow me to introduce myself, Gentlemen. I'm MacGoogle! It was I who released the forgetting gas! You'll never make cheese again! I will RULE THE WORLD! (reconsiders) Well . . . You will never make cheese again! Ha ha ha!

FOREMAN

Excuse me, Mr. MacGoogle, we'll never do WHAT again?

MACGOOGLE

Make cheese—you'll never make cheese . . .

FOREMAN

But Mr. MacGoogle—what exactly is it that you have made us forget?

MACGOOGLE

(Getting annoyed, speaking quickly)
Making cheese! Warming the milk, adding lactic acid bacterial culture, setting the milk so it coagu-

lates and forms a curd. Cutting it, stirring it, heating it, and draining it to separate the whey from the curd, allowing it to mat into one mass, cutting it into slabs, then smaller pieces, salting it, pressing it into forms, then letting it age.

BOSS

Thank you, Mr. MacGoogle! Now we all know how to make cheese again!!

The workers cheer. They sing and dance around MacGoogle, who stands with his arms crossed, glaring.

MACGOOGLE

Drat! Drat! Drat! You'll pay for this!

The workers, in celebration, do a choreographed dance and sing the song from *Godspell*.

WORKERS

(singing) Prepare ye the way of the Lord . . .

*****

Plumbing Store

A plumbing supply store. A long line of people. JIM and WICK behind the counter.

JIM

Yes—I think we have that. I'll be back in just a minute.

Goes down the stairs—fairly obviously faking it.

WICK

I need to get that from the basement.

He also goes down the stairs. The customers wait for a while. Finally one leans over and checks. We see that the two guys are lying there on the ground and playing Monopoly.

> **CUSTOMER**
> Uh—guys? There's a long line here.

> **JIM**
> We're getting your part sir—we'll have it for you in just a minute.

> **CUSTOMER**
> You're not getting our part. You're not even in the basement. There is no basement.

> **WICK**
> Oh—and I guess you're beyond reproach.

*****

Pear Carver

(with Michael Ian Black)

SAM PARKS, a luminous millionaire, sits in his well-appointed Depression-era office. FRED, a young businessman, barges in.

> **FRED**
> Mr. Parks! Sam Parks!

> **SAM**
> What is it, young man, I'm very rich!

> **FRED**
> In a word—"Pear Carver"

> **SAM**
> (wistfully)
> Pear Carver . . .

Music starts.

FRED

I've got an invention! Carves pears out of stone!

SAM

These stone pears, can you eat 'em?

FRED

No—they're stone. But they look just like pears.

SAM

Tell you what—how can I see this, this Pear Carver?

FRED

(excited)

Oh yes sir, Mr. Parks—I've got it right here.

He produces a small knife.

SAM

That looks just like a regular knife!

FRED

Yes sir—you are as smart as you look in the news-reels, sir, that's exactly what it is—it's a small paring knife.

SAM

Well, what kind of stone can you cut with that?

FRED

Super-soft stone, sir. (pause) Like soap, for example.

SAM

(rises)

Sir—soap is no stone.

FRED

Oh no? Then what do you call this?

He produces a rectangular stone.

> SAM
>
> Why, that looks just like a bar of soap, but it's made entirely of stone!

> FRED
>
> Now that I've got your attention, maybe you'd like to see my butt.

> SAM
>
> I'll confess to you now how tired you're making me so that maybe you'll go away.

> FRED
>
> Nothin' doin'.

> SAM
>
> How about ten dollars?

> FRED
>
> Okay. With tax and tip it's about twelve.

> SAM
>
> All right, well, let's just both pay six.

> FRED
>
> That seems fair.

> SAM
>
> Enough small talk. How many pear carvers can you make in a week?

> FRED
>
> Equal to the number of small knives as I can buy.

> SAM
>
> I'll give you two dollars not to take that idea anywhere else.

FRED

But what's in it for me?

SAM

You'll get great exposure, and the money! All the money! Canadian money!

FRED

Do I have to exchange it at Niagara Junction?

SAM

Yes, you'll get it weekly in Commonwealth checks, which you can exchange at any branch of the Bank of Canada.

FRED

Okay, see ya.

SAM

Later, dude. Wait, one more thing!

FRED

What?

SAM

See ya later, dude.

*****

Foot Switch Trailer

Open on a shot of a cute boy in a kitchen.

VOICEOVER

This is Mikey. He's a regular ten-year-old kid.

MIKEY

Dad, can I go to the stork show with Bobby?

VOICEOVER

This is Mikey's dad—

DAD

No! Go to your room!

A shot of them both going off in different directions, mumbling.

MIKEY

I wish he'd give me a chance . . .

DAD

What the hell is a stork show?

VOICEOVER

They just couldn't seem to understand each other, until one night—

Cut to them asleep in separate rooms, split screen. There is a glow and a hum around each of their feet.

Cut to morning, MIKEY gets out of bed, looks down and sees that his feet are large and hairy.

MIKEY

Ahhhhh . . .

DAD gets out of bed, his feet are small and soft.

DAD

Ahhhh . . .

Cut to them meeting in the breakfast room.

DAD

I've got your feet!

MIKEY

and you've got mine!

VOICEOVER

When their feet do the switcheroo, Mikey and his dad don't know what to do.

ROCK MONTAGE:

—DAD tries to drive to work with tiny feet.

—MIKEY walks into school with huge business shoes.

—DAD has feet crossed on desk when associate comes into office; DAD pulls his feet away.

—MIKEY bowling with his friends. He has huge bowling shoes.

—MIKEY jumping hurdles with his classmates. His feet knock over every hurdle.

—DAD getting his feet caught in a street grating . . .

Cut to: DAD is working under the car so only his feet (Mikey's) are showing.

> **MOM**
>
> Mikey! Get out from under the car!

> **DAD**
>
> Don't get excited, Honey, it's me, your husband.

> **MOM**
>
> Don't play games, Mikey, I know those feet any-where.

> **DAD**
>
> You don't understand—it's me, it's me, I just have Mikey's feet.

> **MOM**
>
> Prove it.

DAD remains under the car.

> **DAD**
>
> Remember our wedding night, we were in the hotel in Niagara falls, and we did the Nasty?

MOM

Ed! It is you.

A shot of DAD and MIKEY walking arm in arm.

VOICEOVER

Sometimes, in order to understand someone, you've got to walk a mile in his shoes . . .

DAD

I'll never yell at you again.

MIKEY

I love you, Dad.

Pull out to reveal they are in an outdoor theater. A HOST is showing lots of storks. . . .

VOICEOVER

It's "Swappin Hoofs," coming soon.

HOST

You liked that stork? Take a look at this stork!

*****

David Wain is the director and cowriter of *The Ten*, a 2007 feature film about ten stories, each inspired by one of the Ten Commandments, and the 2008 feature film *Role Models*. His first film, the cult classic summer camp comedy *Wet Hot American Summer* was released in 2001. In television, he created/directed/wrote/acted in two series: *The State* on MTV, and *Stella* on Comedy Central. He lives in New York. www.davidwain.com

The Nature of My Universe As It Relates to Kevin Spacey

Adrianne Frost

I tend to take my reality, twist it, turn it, and try to make it "better." And, even though my reality is pretty damn good, I dream of what I think are better things. I try desperately to get these things. One of those things was Kevin Spacey. I tried to "get" (in the woo sense) Kevin Spacey, so he could "get" me (in the understanding sense) and we could "get" together (in the *Love Boat* sense).

May 20th, 1999, The Meet-Kevin-Spacey Scheme. I was going to meet Kevin Spacey. I *had* to have one conversation with him after being completely wowed by his performance in *The Iceman Cometh*. I had a three-step plan:

Step One: I wrote a witty and perversely verbose letter to Kevin. It was filled with my usual endearing humor, yet tinged with mature praise. I even used the word "enkindled." I typed it in the ever-pleasant and non-threatening Arial font and saved it under fan.doc.

Step Two: I created an invoice for Evergreen Florist, using the invoice template in Word. This shop, of course, does not exist, nor does Anita, the employee who filled the order. The recipient of the delivery: Mr. Kevin Spacey. The time to be delivered, 7:00 P.M.

Step Three: I went to a real florist and bought floral foam and two cheap bouquets of flowers. Back at the apartment, I used an old vase to create an arrangement.

Step Four: As our printer was broken, I went to the printing store down the street and tried to print out the letter. The file refused to open.

Step Five: I ran home, popped in the disk, and found the file was fried.

Step Six: I screamed, "Shit, piss, motherfucker!!!!!!"

Step Seven: I pulled out my lovely Monet *Water Lilies* stationery and decided to handwrite the letter. I looked for my good, letter-writing pen, couldn't find it, and settled for a red felt-tip.

However, because I did not pre-plan *this* letter, it was not half as witty as the first. I was in a hurry and scribbled something I deemed charming and anyone else would deem psychotic. When I was finished, I sealed it and put it into the floral arrangement. I invited Mr. Spacey to dinner for that evening or the next evening. I gave him two options, because I understood how busy he was and wouldn't he appreciate that and wouldn't that appreciation lead to understanding and dinner with me?

You see how this works? IT TAKES OVER.

Step Eight: I wrapped the flowers in pink cellophane—which was *all I had*—and prepared to staple it *professionally* with the invoice on the front.

Step Nine: I searched for the stapler. I couldn't find it. It was now 7:30. I needed to make this delivery. I couldn't deliver it too late, Evergreen's business depended on it! So, I Scotch-taped it together. I might as well have written the fucking letter in red crayon with my non-dominant hand. "A gift from a very special child."

Step Ten: I realized I was seven steps over the three-step plan.

Step Eleven: I was close to finishing and tears when I heard the key in the lock. I was busted. I explained the whole plan to my boyfriend.

Referring to my overalls and t-shirt, he said, "Is that what you're wearing?"

"Yes." *Ass!* "I want to look like a delivery person."

"But what about when you meet with Kevin?"—and God love him for thinking I would. "Don't you want to be dressed up?"

"But I want to look like a delivery person or it won't work!" I whined.

"Honey, don't you think that's going—"

and I swear he said this

"*a little too far?*"

So, creating a floral shop, faking an invoice, inventing an employee, writing a fanatical letter in red (the team color of stalkers), creating a floral arrangement, and planning to deliver it was *okaaaayyyy*, but dressing up like a delivery person was *all fucked up!*

Step Twelve: I dressed up nicely, not too sexily, not too threatening, but not pristine; hint of makeup, minimal jewelry, hair down . . . perfect.

Step Thirteen: I got rid of the steps altogether.

I went to the theater around 10:30 P.M. incognito (read: sunglasses). The #1 Popi was standing outside the theater with some bodyguards. I gave the flowers to one of them. Then, I was speeding away to await my dinner with Kevin.

I imagined we would have witty exchanges about plays we'd been in and mishaps we'd endured on the stage. My heart was pumping as I snuck to the restaurant and had coffee, waiting for the Iceman.

Oh, God, what was I going to do when he walked through that door? Would I gush like a teenybopper, saying things like "awesome" and "cool"? Would I be a serious actor (calling myself so, not "actress," because that's how it is in the "biz"), talking about O'Neill, Mamet, and Chekhov? Would I be flirtatious, coquettishly accepting the orchids from a hothouse in Spain he laid upon the table?

Would I show him my tits?

No matter. He wasn't coming.

Fuck all this bullshit. I'm getting on with my life.

The next week, I waited in the restaurant from 11:30 P.M. to midnight. The Little Engine That Could chugged through me: He's coming, he's coming, he's coming. My life was going to change tonight. This was my break, this was my destiny, this was my fate . . .

Fate decided Kevin was not going to show up *again*.

I held my head high. I slowly walked outside and then I saw it: a big, black 4x4, and Kenny, the #1 Popi, was in the front seat. It was parked outside of Joe Allen's restaurant. I knew Kevin was inside. This was it. I couldn't breathe. I couldn't move. What do I do? What do I do? He was five steps away from me.

I'm goin' in.

I slipped in the doorway. The maitre d' had stepped away from his post. Cool. I mingled with the "after theatre" crowd, scanning the faces for those round eyes, the dimples, the lined features. There, at the bar, beneath a baseball cap and enveloped in a $3,000.00 suit, was Kevin Spacey. He looked relaxed, comfortable, and, most importantly, approachable. He was handsome, liquid cool. My eloquence and wit, not to mention my presumption, were going to serve me well. "Hello," I rehearsed silently, "I'm Adrianne Frost and a great admirer of your work. You've inspired me to write a one-woman show about my life that I would love to share with you. May I join you for dinner? Your treat." (Ha ha—there was the wit . . . "Good, good, good!") I straightened my hair. I pushed through the crowd.

I'd wasted too much of my life on bullshit. Bullshit jobs, bullshit endeavors, bullshit relationships, bullshit, bullshit, bullshit. It took *three* times through rehab to keep me clean and sober. $19,000 a pop. I should've known it wasn't going to work the first three times. When I got the bill, I kept thinking how fucked up I could get on $19,000. Now, I know I wouldn't be the effervescent, loveable mess you see before you now had I not led a completely bullshit existence, and here I was caught up in a (dare I say it?) *bullshit obsession!* (No offense to Kevin Spacey, but this was a bullshit obsession. *As if* he even got the flowers, *as if,* if he *did* get them, he wasn't laughing his nine-million-dollar-a-picture *ass off* while simultaneously reading it to his cast mates and *as if* he'd actually meet with an overgrown, overweight, overzealous fan who was writing a play entitled *The Nature of My Universe As It Relates to Kevin Spacey*!) I was really mad at myself for not having a purpose. Not finding a purpose. It was just success I wanted. Not the work. Not the drive. Just the cheesecake. No baking.

Kevin was facing the bar.

I whispered, "Excuse me." Nothing. I cleared my throat. "Excuse me," I said again. He reached for his beer. I gently tugged on his sleeve and said, "Excuse me."

He turned to face me, uninterested, uninviting.

"Yeeeeeeeeeeeeeeeees?" He grabbed his draft beer from the bar.

I clutched his hand as he shook mine. I couldn't breathe, I couldn't speak. You know how, sometimes, on *Three's Company*, Jack Tripper would be excited to meet someone, like a chef or something (because that's what Jack wanted to be), and Jack would just keep shaking their hand and people watching the show would say, "Oh, that's silly! Silly John Ritter, the slapstick comedian, nobody does that when they meet somebody they admire."

Yes, yes, they do.

He looked at me like a puppy looks at you when you first bring it home (tilting his head to one side). One of his friends eyed me from behind him, like a frat boy eyes the fat girl at a kegger. Kevin was the president of Alpha Psi Spacey. No doubt my nickname around the house was "Tiny."

"Um, um, um, er, er . . ." Then I blurted out, "I'm Adrianne."

He said, "And?"

"Uh, uh, uh . . ."

Brilliant! You fucko.

What was I to say?

"Hi, I'm the girl who sent you flowers and a letter that you probably didn't get because your assistant burned them and I know I seem insane *right now*, but I'm a really nice person and so please be nice to me or I'm gonna feel really shitty and, even though it won't be your fault, I'm going to be depressed all weekend if you don't talk to me in a respectful and decent manner. You see, Mr. Spacey, this is the reason people shoot up entire Luby's cafeterias full of patrons. They create fantasies in their heads about famous people to escape their own pain. Then they meet the celebrities and the celebrities are assholes to them. They empty a round of bullets into Mr. and Mrs. Finkel having fish and Tater Tots in a red vinyl booth. I hope you're not afraid, because I would never hurt a fly and I just want you to *like me*. My mental health kind of depends on it!?"

Instead, I mumbled, "Uh, uh. I'm writing a show that kind of involves you."

He put down his beer and looked me in the eyes, "You're writing a show that kind of involves me? Do I know about it?"

Everyone in the bar and the restaurant and the vicinity of Hell's Kitchen was staring at me. A block away, they stopped the curtain call at *Les Miz* to silence the theater and listen.

I am not usually meek. I have balls of steel. But I shyly answered him, "No."

The maitre d' stuck his face over my right shoulder and reached over me to tap Kevin, letting him know his table was ready.

I expected one of Kevin's friends to shout, "Dude, c'mon, we gotta go to the bonfire. Sorry, Tiny, we gotta motor."

No, no, no, wait, I have more to say!

"Uh, oh, ah, wah, I'd love to talk to you about it sometime," I sputtered.

"The show you're writing?" Kevin asked.

Did he truly seem interested? *Yes! Yes!* He was interested! He wanted to sit with me, talk with me, show me his Oscar, cook me huevos rancheros, read Dr. Seuss to me until I fell into a peaceful sleep, dreaming of Sneeches!

Noooooooooooooo. The smell of desperation permeated the fibers of his Italian suit like onions into tear ducts.

You know, a simple "Yes" would have sufficed. However, my history of expounding on the word "Yes" is legendary.

And so, when Kevin Spacey asked if I wanted to discuss the play I was writing that sort of involved him, where a simple "Yes" would have sufficed, I said, "About the show, theater, life in general."

I will never forget Kevin Spacey's reply as long as I live. With a smarmy thumbs-up and a swift turn-around, he said: "I'd love to, but right now, right now"—and here's where the thumbs-up came—"I'm with pals." And he turned his back. Fwoooop!

Kevin Spacey gave me his back.

You know those horror movies where a person is at the end of the hall and suddenly the hallway gets *reeeeaaaally* long. I was the speck at the end of the hall. Five miles to the exit of Joe Allen's. He turned. Fwooooop!

With each word, my heart broke: "Right," crack, "now," crack, "I'm," crack, "with," crack, "pals," crack, crack, CRACK!

Fucking idiot!

I turned toward the door and the people around me evolved into thirty-foot-tall animatronic clowns, rolling around with their hands on their bellies, laughing, like the Country Bear Jamboree at Disney World. The lens zoomed in and out on their evil grins, as their faces melted together like crayons left in the back of a car. I wanted an "Eat Me" cookie.

Oh, Kevin.

I tried to keep my head up in the face of indignity. I went to a pay phone and called my boyfriend.

"Guess who I just met?" I said.

"Kevin Spacey?" He was thrilled for me.

"Yes, and he was *mean to me.*"

"Oh, honey," my boyfriend lamented. "Where are you?"

"I'm on a pay phone," I pouted. "And now I'm going to have pie."

"Oh, honey, come home."

"No, I'm going to have pie." Pout. "By myself." Pout, pout, pout.

"Come *home,*" he said, gently. "We can have pie here at home."

I hung up the phone and scowled in the direction of Joe Allen's. I wanted to go back in and sit at the bar, show Kevin Spacey that I was better than him, better than the insult I had just received. But all I really felt worthy of was pie.

I had my pie.

There was crust, apples, and cinnamon oozing from every orifice. Have some pie. Food makes things better. Become one with the pie. I became one with the pie. The key to eating a whole pie is to just *eat the whole fucking pie.* Don't think, "Mmmm, should I have pie? How much pie should I have?" Just eat the fucking pie. Eat it. Sometimes I like to pretend I am very tiny and trapped in the pie and I have to eat my way out. "Help, I'm in a pie."

I hated him.

And a few months later, when Brian Dennehy won the Tony over Kevin Spacey, I stood, pie in hand, and shouted, "GOOD!"

I'd like to say something profound, like, "I became a woman the day I met Kevin Spacey." I was already a woman.

Whether or not I see Kevin Spacey again to ask him why . . . I don't know if I really *care*.

Right now, I've dropped anchor. Right now, *this* is the order of my universe.

I no longer anticipate his next film or interview so enthusiastically; I don't snatch up copies of the magazine he's on; I don't visit the websites for the latest news. I don't imagine the next time I spot him on the streets of New York, tackling him and smothering him with praise and kisses. I don't imagine I'll run into him at some swank party after I've won my third Emmy and he'll tackle *me* and smother *me* with praise and kisses and I'll be like Julia Roberts in *Pretty Woman* when she goes back into the store where they wouldn't wait on her and I'll say, "Did you know you turned your back on me once? Big mistake . . . big mistake."

Well, maybe I imagine that a little . . .

Adrianne Frost was a panelist on VH-1's *Best Week Ever* for two years. She recently appeared on *Law and Order* as Public Defender Lois Schwartzenberg and on NBC's *30 Rock*. Her first humor book, *I Hate Other People's Kids*, was published by Simon & Schuster in March 2006. Previously, she appeared on Comedy Central's *The Daily Show with Jon Stewart* and was one of the stars of TNN's *Lifegame*. Adrianne has appeared on NBC's *Late Night with Conan O'Brien*, Fox's *Good Day Live*, NBC's *Law and Order: Criminal Intent* and *Law and Order: Special Victims Unit*. She has also appeared on NBC's *The Today Show*, CNN's *Showbiz Tonight*, *The Glenn Beck Show*, and is one of the permanent guest co-hosts on *The Jay Thomas Show* on Sirius Satellite Radio. In 2004, Adrianne's work was published in *The Signet Book of American Humor*. She is currently working on her second book.

Cleveland Vice

Dave Hill

This article was originally written in 2002 for *FHM UK* Magazine, which—as the name suggests—is the British edition of the popular magazine for dudes. It was to be the first installment of a short-lived (i.e., it ran a total of one time before being mercifully and wisely killed) column I wrote for the magazine called "The Ugly American." The idea was for me—the ugly American in question—to engage in assorted sophomoric and grotesque behavior (often at the risk of catching a disease and/or injuring my testicles) and then report my findings. Because I am shameless and also really needed the money at the time, I figured I'd give it a shot.

To get the ball rolling, the magazine's editors sent me a list of assignments to choose from, ranging from "shagging a fattie" to "shagging a crackhead" to injecting my testicles with saline (a trend of some sort, I was told). The only reasonable option on the list was to spend the evening with a police vice unit. It was a fun assignment and something in which I was genuinely interested. When I handed in the final piece, however, it was deemed "too tame" by the editors, presumably because at no point in the story did anyone touch my goods. In the end we settled on another story to kick off the column. And no—I won't tell you what that one was about.

If there's anything in life I just can't get enough of, it's crime fighting and dangerous women. More often than not, however, I find myself without enough of either. I called my friend Mark, a sergeant for the Cleveland, Ohio, police department, in hopes that he might be able to somehow remedy the situation. He suggested a night of hot crime-fighting action with the Cleveland police vice unit might do the trick and quickly made arrangements for me to tag along with them the following Friday evening.

Like most Americans, my knowledge of police vice units pretty much consisted of whatever I might have picked up from old episodes of *Miami Vice,* so I couldn't help but assume my night on the job would probably turn out to be just another excuse to put highlights in my hair and run around in a pastel suit for a few hours.

I was mistaken.

For starters, Rob insisted that I shy away from my usual fashion instincts and instead try to dress like a "regular" guy for a change; "regular" in this case meaning the kind of guy who smokes crack and has sex with transvestites on a regular basis. Most guys who work on the vice unit try to blend in with their surroundings. Rob also warned me not to "get all giggly" around the other cops, but that's probably because he knows how I can get when forced to say things like "How much for a blow job?" out loud.

At 5:30 P.M. that Friday, I pulled up to the Thirteenth District police station in Cleveland. I had my regular guy look in place: a hooded sweatshirt and jeans ensemble I'd somehow hoped would give me the look of a desperate man in search of good times. I also rubbed some grease into my hair for dramatic effect. I thought it might suggest an air of lawlessness or something, but instead it made me look more like someone who sold discount menswear. I probably should have gone with a hat. To complete the look, I tucked a pack of Camel Lights into my sleeve. I'm not the best smoker, but I figured a few drags paired with a furrowed brow and distant gaze might get me through those moments when my crime-fighting skills failed to shine.

Once inside the station, I was greeted by John, forty-six, a twenty-year veteran of the force and sergeant in command of the district vice unit. Together with his crew of six officers, John hits the streets of Cleveland's West Side most nights of the week to battle the prostitution, drugs, gambling, and liquor violations that are all the rage in this largely run-down section of town. Last year alone, John and his men handed out six hundred felony charges, obtained fifty-five search warrants, and recovered millions of dollars worth of drugs and illegal weapons.

John led me upstairs to his office, a tiny space filled with battered steel desks, bulletproof vests, and more Polaroids of prostitutes than the average person tends to keep at the workplace.

"There's no Crockett and Tubbs here," John explained, beating me to my first question.

Almost on cue, two of John's crew entered the room—Nick and Todd, both scruffy-looking detectives in their mid-thirties. Introductions were made and the two began making me feel right at home by letting me get a good look at one of their guns for a second, a .38 caliber Smith & Wesson that filled me with an uncontrollable urge to use the word "motherfucker" repeatedly in a sentence.

I was then instructed to throw on a bulletproof vest and official vice unit jacket and pile into John's car to begin the evening's festivities.

"Whores are mostly looking for crack around here," John said matter of factly as we pulled out of the station. "You can get a blow job for ten or twenty bucks or just give them some crack." Love can be a funny game sometimes.

We cruised the dimly lit streets of the district for about an hour before John turned to me and asked, "You wanna go pick up a whore?" a question I had never been asked by a sober person before. In order to do this, I had to remove my bulletproof vest and vice unit jacket (these things tend to scare off the whores, I was told) and climb into a civilian vehicle with Todd, who handles most of the vice unit's undercover work.

As Lynyrd Skynyrd's "Tuesday's Gone" played on the radio, Todd and I slowly tooled around while doing our best to look like the saddest two-man bachelor party on the planet. Before long we spotted Felicia, a six-foot-tall, 155-pound African-American transvestite making her way down Cleveland's Detroit Avenue.

"Hey, baby—you wanna party?" I hollered in her direction. I had always dreamed of saying something like, "Who's got the paperwork on you—cuz I wanna sign up?!" if I ever got into this type of situation, but Todd had me convinced that line about wanting to party was the way to go under the circumstances. He was right. After luring her in with the promise of free cigarettes and almost certain premature ejaculation, Felicia was sitting in the back of our car saying things like, "I suck a good dick," and, "I can do both of you," a whole lot more than most people do when they first meet somebody.

With Felicia in tow, we drove a few blocks while Todd negotiated the finer points of getting me a blow job. I tried to act really excited while secretly repeating the words, "Just because you let a large transvestite named Felicia touch your penis while you're out fighting crime doesn't make you gay," in the event that my undercover work got any more demanding.

I let out a sigh of relief as we pulled around to the back of a nearby gas station where John sat waiting to make the bust. We screeched to a halt and John yanked Felicia out of the backseat and slapped a pair of handcuffs on her, at which point she quickly turned into Marcus, a 29-year-old aspiring computer programmer from Pittsburgh who wanted nothing more than to go home to his apartment for the rest of the night. For the past ten years, Felicia/Marcus has been pleasing as many as ten customers a night at an average of $30 a pop. Barring any vacation time, that's roughly 36,500 awkward goodbyes to you and me. Tonight, Marcus would get off with a warning. Sometimes a girl deserves a little break.

While Marcus faked his way in the direction of home, Todd and I made our way back onto the street in search of more action. We drove just a few blocks before Todd spotted a couple of teenage boys in heavy down jackets standing in front of a convenience store. "There's a couple of dope boys," Todd explained before saying those words I'd been waiting to hear all night: "You wanna buy some crack?"

Todd wheeled slowly into the store's parking lot and yelled out, "What's up? You got a twenty for me?"—street lingo for, "I'd really like to purchase twenty dollars worth of crack cocaine from you two young men." Clearly suspicious, the two young men weren't budging. Todd pleaded with them a few more times while I sat silently in the passenger seat trying to look like I had a taste for the rock but mostly thinking about how much I wished I hadn't taken off that bulletproof vest.

We ended up giving up and driving away, but Todd—convinced the two teens had drugs on them—radioed over to John, Nick, and his partner Randy and encouraged them to investigate further. As it turned out, Todd's instincts were right again. ("It's like I got a crystal ball," he explained.) One of the two youths, a pudgy fourteen-year-old African-American named Anthony, was holding three rocks of crack in his mouth when they caught up with him a few minutes later.

"That kid was a fucking human Pez dispenser," John later told me. It's not uncommon for crack dealers to keep the drugs in their mouths so they can swallow them quickly if police should suddenly appear. Unfortunately for Anthony, his technique wasn't quite down yet.

Todd and I were about to stop back at headquarters when he got a call from the Cleveland police strike force unit, who were in hot pursuit of two armed-robbery suspects. Todd slammed his foot on the gas pedal, and before I knew it, we were ignoring traffic laws in a way I couldn't help but envy. Within minutes, we caught up with the strike force on a nearby stretch of highway, where they already had their suspects, a Hispanic male and a Caucasian male, both in their early twenties and both wearing the baggiest trousers I had ever seen in northeastern Ohio, in cuffs and fighting off tears. It's not often I get to stand so close to armed-robbery suspects without fighting off tears of my own, so I couldn't resist posing for a few pictures with them on the side of the road.

By now I was feeling like a crime-fighting veteran or something, which was good because the real excitement was about to come. Todd and I teamed up with John, Nick, and the rest of the crew and headed over to Cleveland's Tenth District police station where plans were being hatched to raid Wiseguys, a *Sopranos*-inspired strip joint on Cleveland's East Side that's become a favorite among coke dealers in need of a good lap dance. I had been to Wiseguys a couple times before, but never to fight crime. This was going to be good.

Inside the Tenth District police station, a plainclothes officer dished out orders to a roomful of undercover cops, fellow vice unit officers, an entire SWAT team, and a one-man canine unit named Gary. I had my vice unit jacket back on at this point, but something still told me everyone else in the room was well aware that I was not essential to the operation. I considered muttering something about how "the commissioner is breathing down my neck" to help matters, but then I realized that sort of talk might not sound too convincing coming from the only unarmed man in the room.

Our game plan in order, we drove a few blocks away to Wiseguys to let the asskicking commence. The SWAT team—menacingly clad in black fatigues, bulletproof vests, helmets, and goggles—went in first to stop the pole dancing–induced merriment in its tracks. A few minutes later, John, the remaining officers, and I slipped through the club's back door—presumably to avoid the cover charge—to assess the situation.

Inside Wiseguys, I discovered a moment stopped in time. The club's once-booming sound system had been silenced, disco balls hung motionless overhead, and ice cubes melted slowly in abandoned cocktails while bikini-clad strippers sat shivering at the foot of an empty stage and disconcerted patrons huddled around small tables while doing their best to hide behind barely lit cigarettes and ill-advised goatees.

For the next couple hours, my new cop buddies combed every inch of Wiseguys, its employees, and its patrons, making fourteen arrests altogether on charges ranging from drug and illegal firearms possession to outstanding arrest warrants. I did my part by pacing the entire club in silence, making note of the countless fashion violations that would go unpunished this evening while taking satisfaction in knowing that—more often than not—allowing someone to walk through life with an open shirt and exposed gold chains tends to provide its own form of justice in the end. I also discovered there was no soap in the men's room, but I decided to keep that bit of injustice to myself.

As I stood waiting for John and his partners to wrap up their endeavors, a stripper with fried blond hair and caked-on mascara turned to me and said, "I'm sure I know you from somewhere," thus signaling it was time to go. I piled back into the front seat of John's car to head back to the station for the last time. As John rehashed the evening's events with Troy, the youngest member of his crew at thirty years old, I sat waiting for that freeze-frame that always comes at the end of all the best cop shows. It never came. Then again, that's the thing about crime fighting—sometimes it just ain't what you'd expect.

Dave Hill is a writer, performer, and musician living in New York City. He has written for the *New York Times, Huffington Post, Salon, Blender,* and the *Cleveland Plain Dealer* among others. He has appeared on VH1, MTV, HBO, Mojo TV, and a bunch of other channels. For more info, check out www.davehillonline.com.

Rejected Jokes from *SNL*'s "Weekend Update"

Jane Borden

Some say that *Saturday Night Live*, after years of being dismissed as hackneyed and irrelevant, is entering another golden age. Is it a coincidence that the show turned around right at the time I joined the list of freelance joke writers for "Weekend Update"? It is, of course, not a coincidence at all. That was sarcasm, one of many tools I use as a master of mirth and joke sorcerer. In other words, I'm really, really good at words. If the pen is mightier than the sword, then my pen is an AK-47. I would credit my ability to distill major world events into pithy punch lines as a gift from God, except that would give him too much credit. The *SNL* gig basically works like this: A producer reads the news (newspapers, magazines, newscasts), and emails the "faxers" a few dozen current headlines per day. Then, on Thursdays, we respond with jokes. I've been on this list for three seasons, which means these facile fingers have released approximately six hundred pieces of coruscating comedy into the world. (I can also do math.)

But only one of my jokes has ever been picked to air. "What?" you are probably wondering. "If she's so great, why so much rejection? And if she doesn't get jokes on the air, how can she take credit for getting the show where it's at?" First of all, please don't end a wonder with a preposition. Secondly, it's true: my contribution has been small. But you've forgotten the adage about a butterfly flapping its wings and causing a hurricane. I haven't forgotten that adage—because I wrote it.

Did you ever consider that my work was cast aside for being too good? Or too smart? Remember the *Monty Python* sketch about a joke so funny it kills everyone who hears it? My jokes are so funny they spontaneously create SARS. I'm wearing a mask right now. And you should be, too. Just because my submissions don't air, that doesn't mean they aren't framed on the writers' room wall as an example of how it's done (next to a "Hang in there!" kitten poster—which I also wrote). Did you just get SARS?

But since you are so desperate to know why my jokes don't make it on the air, I did some amateur sleuthing at 30 Rock and found out exactly what happens between the time my submissions are received and the time they are forsaken.

Cut to any given Thursday. The producer is tired from staying up all night in anticipation of receiving my submission. I take a break from punching up the Bible to send it in. He receives it—an all-staff email goes out immediately: "Jane's jokes are here! They're in!" The entire show gathers in a conference room where the producer reads them aloud for morale-boosting entertainment.

Action figures of Jon Bon Jovi and Richie Sambora will be available this fall. Every few years, the exact same dolls will be given new hair styles and released again.

Monday was Martin Luther King Day. Or as it's known in the South, Monday.

China state television has started shooting a forty-part television series about Bruce Lee. It will end mysteriously at episode 32.

A former secretary at a financial firm has filed a 24-million-dollar lawsuit against her boss, saying he forced her to be his sexual liaison, setting up dates for him, lining up accommodations for his sexual activities, and calling her his "Pussy Coordinator." According to her case, she told him several times she preferred "Pussy Administrator."

Government scientists have created a vaccine against the catastrophic Spanish flu virus of 1918–1919, raising hopes that a remedy could be developed if a modern strain of avian flu turns equally deadly. Unfortunately, however, there is still no antidote to Spanish Fly.

A new study suggests that tai chi, the ancient Chinese martial art, may help prevent shingles. It's already been discovered to prevent girlfriends.

Oprah Winfrey took time out from her fiftieth birthday party to thank the hordes of fans who gathered outside the gates. Then she ate them.

Everyone laughs for five and a half hours straight, but then . . . oh no! They're so far behind! How will they finish the show in time? It is determined that "Update" is forbidden from reading my jokes on the air for fear that audiences would laugh all night, get ill, and call in sick on Monday, thereby causing a national drop in workplace productivity and drive the country into a recession. Sure, my jokes were rejected, but I saved the stock market.

Fast forward to the following week: I am explaining to T. S. Eliot, via Ouija board, my suggested revisions for "The Love Song of J. Alfred Prufrock," when he leads the scope to S, then N, and then L. Oh crap! I forgot it's Thursday! Thanks T. S.—that was close. I owe him one, so I dash off "The Waste Land," hop into a time machine, and give it to him in 1922. Then I crap out a few punch lines, thinking, if I'm not even trying this week, surely they'll be bad enough to not be too good to be accepted.

Australian officials plan to restrict and eventually ban the sale of incandescent lightbulbs in an effort to cut greenhouse gas emissions by four million tons by 2012 and reduce household power bills by up to 66 percent. Fags.

A spokesman for the Mirage Hotel in Las Vegas said that, although they did capture Roy Horn's tiger attack on tape, they will not air the spectacle anytime soon. They're saving it for Fox's reality show, "When Animals Gay Bash."

In a gimmicky departure from the typical ceremony of an English cathedral, a clown will deliver this weekend's sermon while balancing on a wire. The spectacle will continue when the congregation's sins are magically forgiven by a spirit who rose from the dead!

A new interactive Coca-Cola billboard in London's Piccadilly Circus can react to changes in the weather and respond to waves from the street, making it more animated than most British citizens.

Rhonda Grant was fined $165 in Georgia this week for yelling a stream of foul words into the microphone of a drive-thru window at an area Taco Bell. In her defense, she claims she was only reading the menu.

In an interview with Bill O'Reilly, President Bush said that he has no regrets about standing on the deck of an aircraft carrier with a sign behind him declaring "Mission Accomplished," because the sign didn't even refer to the war in Iraq, but rather to his recent trip to the bathroom.

The first same-sex couple in New Jersey was married Monday in Asbury Park. Heh heh: Assbury Park.

And it almost worked. The joke I wrote about Bush made it to the dress rehearsal, but a White House aide was in the audience. When he heard it, he had the Secret Service demand its removal from the live show due to its satirical logic being so crystal clear that it would have finally shown the President the error of his ways, at which point he'd resign. This really stung because, not only did I go another week without getting anything on the show, but also I had already purchased YoureWelcomeAmerica.com.

Time jump to the next week: I'm too busy beating Billie Jean King in tennis to write, so I have the ball boy record the grunts I make while serving, and transcribe them.

Rod Roddy, the announcer on *The Price Is Right,* famous for his line, "Come on Down!" died on Monday at the age of 66. He joins the show's host, Bob Barker, who's been dead for 15 years.

After extensive research, the Illinois Historic Preservation Agency has released a list of quotes falsely attributed to Abraham Lincoln, including the famous lines, "To sin by silence, when they should protest, makes cowards of men," and also, "Whoomp there it is." Repeat: Abraham Lincoln did not say, "Whoomp there it is."

In an effort to avoid the press, Paris Hilton went to a concert this week disguised in a long, brown wig. But she was still spotted because she forgot to disguise her vagina.

Mel Gibson's movie *The Passion of the Christ* is set to be released on DVD. Copies are expected to ascend off of shelves, and then return in three days.

A *Vanity Fair* article said that Bill Clinton struggled to finish his book *My Life* by the deadline. Apparently, he was having trouble with a few of the pages in the Monica Lewinsky section because they were stuck together.

The Who have released two new songs as part of a compilation set of their classic singles. The songs are "Who Are You?" and "No, Seriously, Who Are You?"

A large number of men in the United States who have married or intend to marry mail-order brides are finding their wives barred from entering the United States by a new law intended to give foreign women and the American government more information about the men who place these orders. This is a shame because these women actually are doing the work that Americans don't want to.

Officials in Beijing, who are preparing for the 2008 Summer Olympics, are launching a citywide campaign to discourage offensive local habits, such as spitting in public, public cursing, and pee-peeing in Cokes.

By now, my jokes have garnered so much attention that they are sent directly to Lorne Michael's office. This happens for two reasons: One, he really loves them. And two, he's actually an alien working for NASA, which has been monitoring me. And this is the submission they've been waiting for. He calls the agency and they set in motion plans to transmit my jokes into space as proof of intelligent life on earth.

So you can see that sometimes rejection is actually the biggest form of flattery. You can also see that I am way super-crazy smart. It is suggested that you clip this essay and put it on your fridge for future perusal. But be warned: Neighborhood dogs will cry at the door to be let in so they can hump it.

Writer's note: While fact checking this story, the "Weekend Update" team explained what actually happens when they receive Jane's jokes: "Enh. Anything else?" Also, regarding the one joke that she did get on the air, they said, "Oh, right, yeah. That was a mistake."

Jane Borden is a writer and performer in New York City. Her work has appeared in the *New York Times Magazine, Modern Bride,* and *Time Out New York,* among other publications, and on *Saturday Night Live*'s "Weekend Update," *Tough Crowd* with Colin Quinn, and one of those VH1 talking-heads shows. She's currently writing a book from her Brooklyn apartment.

The El Mocambo Bomb

Kevin McDonald

It was October of 1985. What was? The story I'm about to tell. Christ, don't tell me you're confused already. You really should pay attention.

It was two short months after my comedy troupe, the Kids in the Hall . . . Okay, not *my* comedy troupe—the comedy troupe I'm in . . . Jesus, you're really a stickler for detail.

It was two short months after the comedy troupe I'm in had been "discovered." Long story short, Lorne Michaels had discovered the Kids in the Hall in Toronto. He couldn't have all of us on the show so he hired the two most experienced of us, Mark McKinney and Bruce McCulloch, as writers for *Saturday Night Live*. They had to move to New York.

Now, due to all the attention we were getting, Dave Foley was hired as the lead in a movie where he was promised he would be the Canadian Michael J. Fox. I know, I know. Michael J. Fox *is* Canadian. Will you calm down, for Christ's sake! Anyway, Dave had to move to Vancouver for two months.

There, that's the story.

Not the main story.

Just the story leading up to the main story.

We're going to start the main story now.

Sorry for the delay.

Before the Kids in the Hall were discovered, we had agreed to do a sketch at a big variety show for a frat house in the University of

Toronto. It was to be held at Toronto's famous rock club, the El Mocambo. Where Keith Richards was arrested for doing heroin. Oh, if only we were famous enough to be arrested for doing heroin at the El Mocambo.

It appeared that only Scott Thompson and I . . . or as the troupe lovingly referred to us, "the losers" . . . were in Toronto and able to perform at the El Mocambo show. "Sure, we could do it," thought Scott Thompson and I. "Whether it's all five Kids in the Hall or just the two losers in the hall—the audience is a bunch of college kids. College kids love us!"

When we arrived that night, the show had been on for about an hour. The first thing we noticed was drunk college kids. "All the better. If college kids love us, drunk college kids will love us all the more!" The act on stage was an all-gay choir. The audience loved them. In fact, you could say without fear of exaggeration, the gay choir were killing. "What lovely, tolerant, drunk college kids." If this possibly rowdy crowd was enjoying themselves watching a gay choir, we should be able to go over really well.

We are introduced and with nice, drunk, college kid–applause, we enter the stage and begin our sketch. The sketch involves Scott and me talking "humorously" of how sad I am about the girlfriend who just split up with me. As we talk, I look into the audience and supposedly see my ex-girlfriend sitting with her new boyfriend. This of course is a ruse. We've done this sketch a million times. I just pick a couple that is sitting close to the stage, pretend that the woman is my ex-girlfriend and that she has started dating the "jerk" that she is sitting with.

What usually happens next? In order to get me time alone with the woman, Scott, riding on the wave of uproarious laughter that we most assuredly will be getting, takes the man on stage and hits on him. We've done it a million times. It always works. Only this time, we never get to the part where I get the guy on stage for Scott to hit on him.

To my horror, I have chosen an unnecessarily drunk woman who isn't laughing or playing along like they usually do. She is pushing me and telling me in her best college-educated elocution to "Fuck off!" She goes as far as to look at my unruly, curly hair and call me "Hair Asshole!" She in fact leans right into the mike and calls me "Hair Asshole!" This gets our first laugh. In an obvious attempt to straighten my unruly, curly hair, she begins to pound my head with the mike, over and over.

The audience, now seemingly angry with Scott and me, begin to chant "Fags . . . Fags . . . Fags . . ." Remember, this is a crowd that just gave a gay choir a standing ovation. But at us they're throwing homophobic slurs. I see in the corner of the club that even a couple of members of the gay choir are chanting "Fags . . . Fags . . ."

As I continue to be pummeled by the curly hair–hater, the next act comes on stage. They are a three-piece rock band. Unaware that another act is "performing," they start doing a sound check. An angry Scott, who is still on stage, starts yelling at the bass player. The musician puts down his bass and starts yelling back at Scott.

Meanwhile, the woman that was hitting me is now arguing with her boyfriend. I, a professional coward, decide to quit the performance and I slink off to the bar. No one seems to notice or care. The emcee comes on stage and stands in front of Scott and the bass player who are now furiously pushing each other.

The emcee says it's now time for a contest ". . . and the winner gets this new Billy Crystal album, *Mahvelous!*" The crowd cheers. They love Billy Crystal! Why isn't he here instead of those fags? The emcee continues, "To win, you just have to answer the following question: What song did both the Beatles and the Rolling Stones record?" I spit take my margarita. I know this. I have both albums. My crazy Aunt Mimi gave them to me when she had her second nervous breakdown and was blaming it on rock and roll. "I Wanna Be Your Man," I scream out loud. The emcee looks over the crowd, sees me, pauses, and then smiles. Then he quickly yells out, "We have a winner! Come on stage and get your Billy Crystal album, young man."

I rush onto the stage, I pass Scott and the bass player, now spitting on each other, and go to the emcee. I get my Billy Crystal album. Forgetting that I am "Hair Asshole," the audience applauds. I turn to the audience, proudly holding my Billy Crystal album and tell them, "You look mahvelous!" I get my first laugh of the evening. I pass the bass player, who now has Scott in a headlock as they wrestle around the stage, knocking over the drums.

I return to my margarita and happily sip from it. I scan the world-famous El Mocambo, looking at Scott, the emcee, the gay choir, and the entire crowd. It's true, everyone does indeed look mahvelous.

Kevin Hamilton McDonald was born in Montreal, Canada, and lived there until age seven when his father, Hamilton, a dental supplies salesman, was transferred to Los Angeles, California, and moved Kevin, his mother (a homemaker), and his older sister out there. The family later moved to Toronto, Canada. Kevin has described himself as an overweight, asthmatic child who spent most of his time in front of the TV, studying up on comedy. Kevin began his acting career early, taking theater classes in high school. Kevin later attended Humber College as a theater major, but was kicked out because he could only do comedy. However, one of his teachers enrolled him in the famed Second City improv workshops. His first day, he met Dave Foley and they quickly became good friends. They worked together as ushers in an art house theater and together they joined up with Luciano Casimiri and formed the first incarnation of the Kids in the Hall.

A Little Bad

Meredith Hoffa

In the sixth grade I was flying high.

The size of my face and body had recently caught up to the gigantic size of my teeth, which was super-exciting. I was smiling freely and big. And going through a period of brazenly exploring and developing my personal style.

I discovered, for example, that wearing a long T-shirt (belted) with jellies sandals and no pants was a smart, sexy outfit for any occasion that made me feel like a million bucks. I also discovered that wearing lilac body spray—purchased for me by my Grandma Dorothy on her singles cruise to Bermuda—brought out the feminine lady in me. And I discovered that wearing undies with a leotard is considered dorky, so I started going without and uncovered a delightfully sleek new silhouette much more befitting of the world-class gymnast I planned to become.

I decided I should no longer be a girl who wore turtlenecks with rainbow-colored hearts all over them. Yes, I owned a whole fleet of them, but I limited myself to wearing them twice a week, max. Because what I really needed to do was to forge new ground. And I was doing so—with success. It was an exhilarating time. It felt like all I had to do was have my eyes open and trust my instincts.

I was a gal with numerous interests and hobbies, what my dad proudly called "a well-rounded individual." There was the world-class gymnast thing—plus soccer, ping-pong, running a part-time nail salon out of my friend Nikki's house. Also, I was planning for a career as a TV reporter so I was frequently holed up in my room murmuring news and commentary into my tape recorder. But I had one hobby that overshadowed all the others. By a long shot.

And that hobby was boys.

I loved boys. I'd been a lover of boys for years already, swooning over everything about them: their dirty sneakers, their choppy handwriting, the way they panted "here" in gym class when they wanted the ball. And now, finally, things were heating up to my satisfaction. We were starting to have boy/girl parties. We were writing each other valentines and signing them with the semi-racy *luv*. We were publicizing lists of the classmates we *liked*-liked.

And with my new face-to-teeth proportions, I was so in the mix.

I totally adored all the boys in my grade, but my main boyfriend was a diminutive, brown-haired one named Jacob who was in the highest reading group and could pull off a pastel-colored polo shirt in an unbelievably cute way. Plus he was on TV for a commercial in which he played the son at a family barbeque and talked about "lean meat, heart-healthy meat." Incredible. That I got to be around him and all the Ward School boys every day got me out of bed mornings with a spring in my step. I had so much to live for.

That is . . . until I did something stupid and ruined everything for myself.

I got a bad haircut.

Actually, it was a cool haircut, just not on me.

What I got was one of those super-short skater-inspired 'do's that some adorable, sassy girls were getting in the late '80s: chopped close to the scalp on one side of the head, cut all angular and flopped over the eye on the other. Think: Mary Stuart Masterson in *Some Kind of Wonderful*, but with more asymmetry, kind of along the lines of the blond guy from A Flock of Seagulls.

Now this haircut was no impulse thing. It was part of my grand master plan to continually increase my unique awesomeness. I got the cut because it seemed like the appropriate next step. I got the cut because I had style, it was turning out, and so I needed cool, non-run-of-the-mill hair to match. I got the cut because my instincts so clearly said *go for it.*

But when I chose Mary Stuart Masterson as my hair inspiration, I didn't take into account her smooth, glossy locks and WASPy, naturally skater-y looks. Nor did I take into account my thick, wavy orange hair and Jewy looks and the fact that perhaps deep down I really was a turtleneck-with-rainbow-colored-hearts-all-over-it kind of girl and always would be. Overall, what I didn't take into account was that in trying to pull off this haircut, I might look like a big a-hole.

By the time Frank at Supercuts spun my chair around and went *ta-da,* I was beyond despondent. I'd brought in magazine pictures of MSM for him to use as a guide (a tip from *YM* magazine), but what I saw in the mirror post-haircut was a person who didn't even look like a member of the same species as her. Technically I had The Cut. But . . . it wasn't right on me. I was all wrong.

Supercuts Frank could tell I was about to freak out. He grabbed me by the shoulders and assured me I looked "wicked sexy." His Boston accent exploded everywhere. *"Meh-reh-dith. You hahve gwot to trust me. You look frickin' awe-sum."*

The thing was, I didn't trust him. Yes, Frank was a professional stylist and I was just a sixth-grader. But I knew I had just fucked up and there was nothing he could do to fix it. I'd simply gotten in over my head, not unlike when I went on TWA unchaperoned to New York to visit my Aunt Shelley but had to come home after only a day on account of debilitating homesickness. Unlike the New York trip, though, in this scenario there was no home to go home to.

Frank wouldn't understand all this. He didn't know me. He didn't know that *that very afternoon* I had Shari Finerman's birthday party and I wouldn't be allowed to bail. Oh, Frank. He sent me off with some Vidal Sassoon mousse—for use just on the left side of my head, he reminded me—and as I trudged through Harvard Square to meet my mom's minivan, I scanned people's faces, trying to ascertain what America thought of my new look. Unfortunately, it was raining, so most people were looking down.

In the car, my mom complimented my new hair. My mom, who

for my entire childhood wore her naturally straight hair in a permed, springy dome—with a radius of about half a foot—around her head. I crawled into the way back where I spent the drive home watching the windshield wipers and trying to figure out how someone as smart as me could have been so wrong.

Shari Finerman's birthday party was at Sammy White's Brighton Bowl. Shari was infamous in my grade for her mucousy crying fits during math, but still, her party was highly anticipated. It was boy/girl. Normally I'd be foaming at the mouth with excitement and Nairing the crap out of my legs, but today . . . let's face it, I was in crisis. I shut myself in my room and whispered soothing thoughts into my tape recorder and eventually grew calm enough to focus on the task at hand: dolling up.

Obviously I'd wear my go-to cool ensemble, a Benetton outfit that encased me in fire-engine red from head to toe: a thick, red, cotton sweatshirt with "Benetton" appliquéd all over it, and on the bottom, wool red-and-green pleated plaid pants that tapered really intensely at the ankle. This was by far my chic-est outfit, not just because of its inherent attractiveness, but also because I'd purchased it with my own babysitting dollars. (My parents were against name-brand clothes like this because why should people be walking ads for clothing companies. As they put it. Lamely.)

Pulling the sweatshirt on over my newly shorn head was a weird sensation and definitely a little disconcerting. But as I sized myself up in the full-length mirror, I wondered if perhaps I felt a little tug of hope . . . ? I looked different, for sure. But . . . maybe not half bad? In fact, between my mod haircut and high-class Benetton outfit . . . I was emitting a rather cosmopolitan vibe. As I posed in the mirror with my hands on hips and one foot pointed out in a tendu, I wondered if perhaps I had never looked more sassy and/or adorable! Before leaving, I smeared Vaseline onto my eyelashes to create dewiness (another tip from YM) and . . . wow. I could've kissed myself.

But then, not long into the party—before the bowling even got underway—my life as I knew it came to a screeching halt. And the shocking thing was, it took only an instant.

I was at the scoring table sorting through my goodie bag when suddenly I became aware that the boys were coming in my direction. They were moving in a kind of traveling clump formation. I didn't have time to wonder what they were doing. All I knew was one moment they were coming and the next moment they were there. And they had something to say. Jacob spoke for them.

"Your haircut is a little bad," he said.

"We don't think you're pretty anymore."

And that was it. They headed off to play Centipede.

The rest of the party transpired in a blur. I did all the stuff. Bowling. Pizza. Presents. Thank God there were no sex games like Spin the Bottle or Truth or Dare because my mind was whirling wild on other things. Foremost among them: I was ugly. *I had made myself ugly.* Yesterday: not ugly. Today: ugly.

"We don't think you're pretty anymore." The worst thing I ever heard. A punch in my rabbit-tooth face. But. That word: *anymore.* Did Jacob's insult also contain the totally mind-blowing compliment that I *had* been pretty? Like, *previously*? I kept trying to wrap my head around this idea, but eventually . . . had to just give up. Because whether I had once been pretty or not, ultimately I had to face the bottom line. The bottom line was that there was attractiveness to be had in the world and I did not have it.

Beginning that afternoon, right there in Sammy White's, I started growing my hair. "Growing hair" is a funny idea if you really think about it. Hair grows, as its default state, and you can either cut it or not. But my hair situation now classified as Emergency; I no longer had the luxury of thinking about hair growth as a passive thing. No. I had to Grow My Hair actively and with purpose. I had to Grow It Hard.

In the days, weeks, and months that followed, I focused with laserbeam intensity on Growing My Hair. There were physical things I did, like pulling it, coaxing it down with a fine-tooth comb, brushing it twenty minutes a night (a tip I learned from *Are You There God? It's Me, Margaret*). I'd twist tiny bits of it into all sorts of clips and bands with the hope that by being accessory laden, the hair would seem long, and if it *seemed* long, then perhaps it would *be* long. And in addition to those physical tactics, I also worked on my hair mentally. Which basically meant just thinking about it all the time.

Yes, growing my hair was my full-time job. But honestly, I didn't resent it. I would've worked on my hair *double* full-time if such a thing existed. I wasn't who I wanted to be. And more importantly, I wasn't who Jacob and the other Ward School boys wanted me to be.

The worst part? I had no one to blame but myself.

Winter was long.

By spring, my hair had made it into a short bob.

Kind of fucked-up choppy bob, but it was progress. I started wearing the top section in a high, unicornesque ponytail—like an uglier version of Pebbles—and I looked all right, I thought, particularly when I wore my new Esprit crop top (bought with babysitting dollars). The Esprit shirt was a really cool mint-green color and had the added benefit of draping in such a way so as to obscure my disturbing new mini-boobs. Plus, it went nicely with my eyes, which my favorite babysitter Debbie told me were a cool, unique color called hazel.

The game plan was that my hair would level out at my chin by July and then approach mid-collar (upturned) by August. I knew I couldn't count on it happening *exactly* on that schedule, but I was hopeful, and whenever I had a chance to wish on something, like an eyelash or my twelfth-birthday candles, that was what I wished for.

Overall it was an optimistic time. And, actually, I was happy—enough—because I figured that at this rate, I had a prayer of getting pretty in time for junior high. And a prayer, it seemed to me, was good enough to work with.

Meredith Hoffa is a former journalist (most recently with *The NewsHour with Jim Lehrer* on PBS), and is now a writer and performer in Los Angeles. She can currently be heard on XM/Sirius radio's sketch comedy show *A Complete Waste of Time*. She has performed her sketch material at the Groundlings, among other places, as well as in the show "Martinis for Dinner," which she and her writing partner produce and write. Her work has also appeared in *The Boston Globe Magazine*.

Gorilla Cartooning

Todd Rosenberg

After doodling my way through college (and two summer sessions) to a stellar 2.27 GPA and worthless degree in "Communication," I moved home with my parents and hazily announced I was going to be a newspaper cartoonist. They weren't thrilled with the prospect that they just threw a sack of tuition money in the garbage, but were happy that I'd finally found my "calling."

I didn't worry about getting a job. I was going to be successful like my hero Gary Larson, creator of *The Far Side*! I worked day and night on my first comic strip called *The Thymes*. Sort of like *The Times* but with the HY thing. Get it? I was awesomely creative!

I sent it out to newspapers, syndicates, agents, and directly to cartoonists I respected (from a mass mailing compiled from a book called *Humor and Cartoon Markets,* an annual book filled with industry addresses and advice). Then I sat back and researched the best way to field offers. I planned for calendars and greeting cards. All I fielded was rejection letters. I was stunned. I didn't get it. My plan was foolproof! Syndicated newspaper cartoonist! Me! I didn't understand. Rejection? Me? But . . .

Five jobs, twenty extra pounds, four more rejected strips, and thousands of dollars on Rogaine later, I found myself working in the world of book publishing in sales but still trying to be a cartoonist. I'd work at night. I'd work on weekends. I'd work . . . at work. And finally, I had created my masterpiece comic strip called *The 13th Floor*. It was like *The Far Side,* but more edgy. And had social commentary . . . kinda sorta. With a dark side! Perfect!

BRIAN WOULD GROW TO RESENT
HIS FATHER BUT AT THE TIME HE
APPRECIATED BEING THE COOLEST KID
IN THE FOURTH GRADE

I sent my submission everywhere again and the mailing again blew back in my face in the form of stock rejection letters. I couldn't believe it! Did people not know genius anymore? WTF! Officially desperate and angry, I decided that I needed a new self-marketing technique to get my noncareer jump-started. Something that would result in immediate attention . . .

Here was the plan: A full, frontline assault on the *New York Post* (they had a lot of comics in the paper at the time). I took my top twenty *13th Floor* cartoons and photocopied them a hundred times and included a cover page that said, "If you think these cartoons should be in your newspaper, please called the comics editor @ ext. 124" (or whatever it was). A hundred stapled packets. Then I sat in

MANY OF LIFE'S INEXPLICABLE
PROBLEMS BECAME CLEAR TO FRED
AFTER HE WAS WELCOMED INTO
HEAVEN BY THE LORD

AFTER DISCOVERING HIS SON HAD PLANTED
A "PUPPY TREE", SIDNEY REALIZED THE
"BIRDS AND THE BEES" TALK WAS OVERDUE

front of the NY *Post* offices at 8 A.M. and handed my cartoon packet to employees as they headed inside. One special packet with my work phone number was handed directly to the comics editor himself.

Of course, after being blown away by my greatness the comics editor would be swarmed with phone calls—then call me. I imagined his voice mail box filled with gushing praise and people begging to include my cartoons in the *Post*.

For two days there was a long confusing silence—then I received *the* phone call. It was him! He was calling to make an offer, no doubt! He was going to gush praise! I sat back in my cubicle chair with the phone pressed to my shoulder and my hands clasped behind my head and took a deep successful breath.

The guy sounded old. Very old. He asked me if I thought cartoons with blasphemy and murder really belonged in the *Post*. I sat up straight in my chair and held the phone with my hand. Wait? Where was the gush?! He said the word *murder*. All of a sudden, it dawned on me. Absolutely not! They can't do murder! What was I thinking?

Cartoon by cartoon this guy flipped through. Not one laugh. Only requests for explanation of "What's the joke there?" I'd explain. He'd say, "Uh huh." It was humiliating. I stuttered and sweated through the conversation, defending my cartoons but realizing how way off I was.

IT'S IMPOSSIBLE TO PREDICT WHAT THE
FUTURE HOLDS IN STORE FOR SOME CHILDREN,
HOWEVER, IN LARRY'S CASE...THERAPY IS A SAFE BET

When we hung up the phone, I looked around my cubicle and felt like crying and throwing stuff. I was angry. I started to get scared that I was crazy. I had to start all over again. I needed to vent.

Out of frustration I started to create a Post-it note flipbook of some guy getting his head ripped off and blood flying everywhere. Played backwards the head was put back on the headless body and he'd stand there smiling. I played with it back and forth. Back and forth . . . making sure to always end with him smiling.

BUSINESS WAS SLOW

Todd "Odd Todd" Rosenberg created the website oddtodd.com featuring animations about an unemployed guy. The popularity of the website led to the publication of the *Odd Todd Handbook: Hard Times, Soft Couch* by Warner Books and the sale of *Odd Todd: The Movie* to Paramount Pictures. Todd also frequently provides "humorous" animated segments for *ABC World News Tonight, 20/20,* and *PBS*. He lives in Brooklyn with his dog and is currently working on some arguably funny stuff.

Handsome

Lianne Stokes

Let's hear those sleigh bells ring-a-ling ting ting ting a ling too. Ahhh . . . the sweet smell of Christmastime in New York City. On one particular night in December 1999, everything seemed rather normal. Crowds of tourists swarmed and milled about Rockefeller Center, craning their necks to see the top of a giant tree with its lights shining like the great white hope.

I was nestled inside at Rockefeller Center at my first company holiday party. At twenty-three years and eleven months old, I was a newborn baby. Out of college not yet a year, I'd landed my first job at a hulking, gigantic ad agency in midtown Manhattan. I was working as a production assistant, which meant that I used a lot of pink and yellow Wite-Out (who knew it didn't only come in white?) and got blamed every time a "Digibeta" wasn't dubbed correctly. I was just happy to be there. Prior to that I was working as a dental assistant, so making travel arrangements for Heather Locklear's hairdresser and his three assistants was a dream job compared to sucking saliva out of a stranger's mouth with a small plastic tube.

I'd been on the prowl for some time looking for a "man-friend" and was often known to perch myself seductively over the copier like a Jewish-looking, brunette Jayne Mansfield. The purpose of this was to see if an ad guy would want to suck faces with me over a gin and tonic at the local Irish pub. At that age there's no pressure. You meet. You greet. You make out. Had I known that I'd still be alone at thirty this story would have never happened. Herein lies the evidence that time is wasted on the young and crazy.

Inside the dimly lit party I sipped my cranberry and vodka through a thin red straw. Standing there decked out in an all-black outfit with a detachable chinchilla faux-fur collar, I thought my days of struggle were far behind me. With every sip of the tart vodka, another skater wiped out on the ice. This was the omen I didn't heed. Quickly he approached—"He" being my handsomest coworker. A full gestation period apart, he was exactly nine months my senior. We engaged in witty banter that went a little something like this:

> Me: So then Marge said, "Homie!" Then Homer goes, "Dope!"
> Him: I think I've seen that episode.

Fade to black.

Two hours later my handsome coworker and I were drunkenly linked arm in arm leaving the Christmas party to attend what we were told was the "Christmas afterparty." Our coworker Stacy chased after us yelling, "David! Daaavvviddd!!!! You have a girlfriend!" To which David responded, "So what?" My standards mirroring that of a dime-store hooker, I took the ball and challenged Stacy's warning. "Stacy, you're just jealous. Hey, Rita in Accounts Payable, Stacy has a crush on me and she's just jealous . . . riiight?" As I said this I made a V-shape with my index and middle finger and poked my tongue through it.

Cut to a smoky dive bar.

My mascara was smeared and running down my face. I was seated on a bar stool next to "Handsome." His hand was on my thigh and he was whispering into my ear. "I think we'd make a great couple. Me and my girlfriend are so over."

My response: "My dad would love you!"

"Let me get this one," he slurred, summoning the bartender.

Moments later, two cool, frothy Miller Genuine Drafts appeared on the bar. I remembered in a haze other coworkers approaching us and cheering on our love with shots named "The Buttery Nipple" and "A Red-Headed Slut" before slinking back into the night.

When the bill came he asked me if I could pay because his credit card was "demagnetized." When the clock struck 2:30 A.M., we hopped in a cab and headed to his place in Woodside, Queens. The yellow cab raced down the FDR as we slurred our way through some flirtatious, meaningless conversation in the backseat. The cab screeched to a halt and Handsome got out while I paid the driver.

As his fingers turned the knob, I was anxious with anticipation. The door creaked open like a haunted house. My half-open eyes rolled over his bachelor pad. He had no furniture but a mattress on the floor and a hanging portrait of a Native American kayaking down a river. We sat on the mattress and he asked, "Wanna smoke pot?"

"Yeeesss!" I answered.

As we huffed and puffed, I laid my head on his lap. I closed my eyes and pictured myself jumping up and down on the hardwood floors screaming "OMG! OMG! I totally have a boyfriend!" Handsome made a motion for me to sit up. Then he said curtly, "OK, I'm going to bed." He threw me a beach towel that read CHASE BANK and left me alone on the mattress as he slammed the door to his bedroom. I'd been bitten by the love bug. The following morning we took the Number 7 train back to Manhattan and made polite conversation until we reached the elevator.

Six months later.

"Me and my girlfriend are so over" ran on loop in my head. One summer day in June, the company paid for us all to go to Yankee Stadium. After the game we all headed to a local watering hole to shake our moneymakers. Keeping with tradition I slammed a few vodka and cranberries and spied Handsome across the bar. I stormed him. Some say I charged. I wish I'd sauntered. But I stormed like a drunken paratrooper. I got right in his face. And by that I mean I leaned in for the kiss. My luscious, intoxicated lips gleaming with Bonne Bell lip gloss puckered right up in full view of the entire company. My eyes were closed, but I saw his face contort. Then I heard these words:

"I don't remember telling you that I left my girlfriend." People had obviously been talking.

My baby greens popped open. "*What?*"

The record stopped. You could hear a pin drop.

Exasperated, I yelled, "Ha! Well then, you owe me money."

Falling on me, he grabbed my arm and escorted me out of the bar. I remember him promising to take me to a local burrito joint to make it all up to me. Then he threw me in a cab.

Inside the cab I was far from re-creating the ride to Queens. I was crying and alone. Dumped by the fake boyfriend that roamed my head. Suddenly the cab driver broke the monotony.

"Where you go lady?"

Far from my finest hour, I was so inebriated that I couldn't recall my address. I responded, "Take me to a place where I can forget about my life."

"Geeet out!" he screamed. Snapping like a twig he yelled, "You owe two dollar for wait fee."

I handed over the money and things couldn't get any worse. As the cab's tires screeched away, I stared at the asphalt. I decided my next move would be to leave my broken dreams behind me.

My office was only a few blocks away so I decided to sleep there.

Blowing through the revolving door I angrily flashed my Old Navy gift card at two amused security cards.

"Miss, we'll need your identification." One of them laughed.

"I gaaaves it to you." I slurred.

Passing them at warp speed, I jumped into an open elevator. Pressing the button for my floor, I figured I'd sleep it off on my boss's couch. However, I didn't have my security pass, which made it hard to gain access through the large glass doors that separated me and the couch.

Then a drunk bulb popped into my head. The media planners on nine never lock their doors. I raced down the stairwell and surveyed my options. I picked a corner cubicle floor of a junior media planner. Within seconds I threw my purple lightweight jacket down like Sir Drunk-A-Lot and laid my head upon it.

The next morning around eight o'clock I was jolted out of a deep sleep by the beeping of a fax machine. As my eyes popped open, it all came back to me. Handsome's rejection, the Cran 'n' Vodkas, coworkers staring. Oh, the rejection. Popping to my feet I thought not a moment about what a low point sleeping in my office was, but sought to seek revenge. After collecting myself in the bathroom, I took the elevator up to the sixteenth floor. I walked over to Handsome's cubicle and started riffling through his possessions. I opened drawers and found gym socks, M&M wrappers, and alas, a diary, small and black. I tore through its pages. His handwriting like chicken scratch, I could not decipher a thing. However, there was not a sloppy word about me. The only passage I could make out was an entry that read, "Cops came by looking for my brother last night." That's nice. At this point I let it go, lest I be beseeched by a future with a wayward brother-in-law. On my way out I noticed that an autographed copy of the self-help book, *Who Moved My Cheese?* was on top of his computer. Before leaving and closing the doors on this rather pathetic chapter, I made my mark. I stole his autographed copy of *Who Moved My Cheese?* and in its place I left a Post-it note that read, "I did."

Lianne Stokes began performing stand-up comedy in 2001. A few years later she took the next logical step and started a blog. She enjoyed her "Warhol 15" when said blog was linked to *Gawker* (which led to hate mail) and *Consumerist*. She reveled in all the anonymous hate email that it brought. In 2007, she got a day job as an advertising copywriter and went into therapy. Turns out she's not so tough after all.

Losing It

Michael Colton

> I originally wrote this piece, about my mother rejecting me, for *The New York Times Magazine*. My editor said it wasn't right for them, but he passed it on to a producer at *This American Life*, who liked it, bought it, and recorded an interview with my mother about the incident. A few days before the piece was scheduled to air, it got bumped for time. (Technically, they haven't rejected it, so it still might air one of these weeks. Keep listening.) The silver lining is that they gave me the audio recording of my mother's interview, which allowed me to turn the piece into a multimedia extravaganza that I've performed at theaters and colleges across the country. But never in front of my mom.

I was seventeen when my mother disowned me.

This was an unexpected development in our relationship. All through our childhood, she had never grounded me or my twin brother, Brian. Not when we got kicked out of the mall for going up the down escalator; not when Brian drove her car without a license; not even when I came home from a party covered in vomit (my own). She told us dirty jokes she heard at work, let us watch R-rated movies. As long as we got good grades, she didn't care. She was, as far as these things go, a cool mom.

I suppose our misbehavior seemed minor compared to what she had been through with our two older siblings. Their struggles had put our family into therapy. My older sister was anorexic and suicidal; my older brother, tragically, was a bar mitzvah DJ.

But Brian and I were my mother's babies. Even when we were high-school seniors, she still made our lunches every day, in brown paper bags with our names on them. Tuna fish sandwich, an apple, maybe a granola bar. To my mother we were innocent. Until we did *the bad thing.*

During my senior year, I lost my virginity to my girlfriend, Jessica Alba (not her real name). My mother really liked Jessica Alba. She was Ivy-League-bound, her father was a professor at the same university where my father was a professor, and she was the captain of the girls' soccer team, which in suburban Massachusetts made me the equivalent of the girlfriend of a Texas quarterback.

We had talked about losing our virginity for months. This was not a careless, spontaneous act. In fact, she had just written an article for the school newspaper about a pregnant classmate named Chastity, so on the scheduled night, she arrived in my basement armed with five different forms of birth control, two of which I had never heard of.

Six days later, my twin brother lost his virginity with his girlfriend, Shakira. This was not a coincidence. Brian and I had always been competitive with each other. We kept track of who got to first base first, second base second. Yes, I beat him to home plate—not that it matters now. Neither of us has sex anymore. Except for him.

That night, a few hours after Brian had become a man, he and I lay on my parents' bed watching TV. Our father was in the hospital, trying to pass a kidney stone. When our mother came home from work, she joined us upstairs, then entered and quickly exited her bathroom. She looked confused: "What is that in my toilet?" I shrugged and looked to Brian. He laughed, like he always did when he was nervous.

What neither my mother nor I knew yet was that Brian, after losing his virginity in our bedroom that afternoon, had made two mistakes. Mistake #1: He tried to get rid of the evidence by flushing it down the toilet. Mistake #2: He used the toilet in my parents' bathroom instead of ours. Why? Because my parents' bathroom was a good six or seven steps closer than our own bathroom was. As if punishing Brian for his laziness, the plumbing betrayed him.

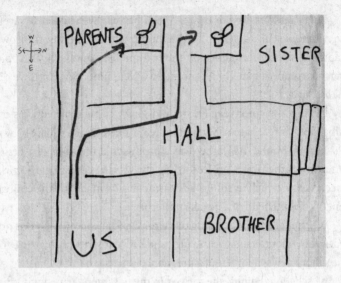

My mother asked again: "What is that in my toilet?"

Brian paused, trying to think of a lie that would make sense: A science experiment? Drug smuggling? Blame it on our friend Steven, whom my mother already hated? Eventually, he settled on the truth. She had never grounded us, right? She'd understand. She's a cool mom. He took a deep breath. "Mom, it's a condom. I had sex with Shakira."

My mother's demeanor did not change. This confession had no impact. It didn't register. It wasn't in English.

She asked again: "What is that in my toilet?"

Brian repeated his answer, and then, never one to brave a storm alone, he blurted out, "And Mike had sex with Jessica Alba!" As if volunteering this irrelevant information would somehow make her feel better.

Finally, something detonated within my mother. Synapses fired. Her physical features changed, eyes sinking back into her skull, wrinkles spontaneously appearing. It was kind of like what happened to the Nazis' faces at the end of *Raiders of the Lost Ark*.

"Get out of my room. I'm going to throw up. Get out of my room!"

We ran out and she slammed the door. I started to yell at Brian for ratting me out, but then her door flew open and she stormed toward us, her eyes ablaze.

"You had sex with those sluts in my house? In my bed?!? Those sluts?"

There was so much I wanted to explain. That her twin sons did not have an orgy in her bedroom. That, in fact, no one had sex with the sluts in her bed. That, frankly, "sluts" is a loaded term. But I couldn't bring up any of this, because I was under attack. My mother accompanied her rant with ear-ringing slaps to our skulls.

"You are not my children! You are not my sons! In my bed? With those sluts? Get out of my house! You are not my children!"

The blows kept coming. Since she had never hit us before, we had no idea she was capable of such a beatdown. Eventually she ran out of steam. She lost her grasp on syntax.

"Sluts! In my house! . . . Not my children! . . . My bed!"

Exhausted, she retreated to her room and pulled the covers over her head.

Later that night, we visited my father in the hospital, where morphine had made him loopy. Normally a quiet scientist, he now greeted us with an IV in his arm and a naughty grin on his face: "I hear you guys have been fooling around!" He turned to a nurse and pointed at us: "They just had sex!"

Unfortunately, it was about a decade before my mother could ever be that casual about what happened. And she's never officially dis-disowned us. For me, as for any teenager, losing my virginity was a desperate wish come true. But for my mother, it was the end of an era.

That next morning was frosty. No words were spoken. Brian and I rushed through breakfast. As we were leaving for school, we opened the fridge and saw that the brown paper bags, usually as predictable as the tides, were not in their usual spot.

"Mom," we asked, "where's our lunch?"

She narrowed her eyes at us. She had stayed up all night plotting her revenge, and she chose her words carefully:

"You're old enough to have sex? You're old enough to make your own lunch."

Michael Colton writes for movies, television, and magazines. He appears regularly on VH1's *Best Week Ever* and was the co-founder of the now-defunct Web magazine *Modern Humorist.*

Letterman or Conan

Wendy Spero

It was senior year of college and I was frantically trying to figure out what I should to do with the rest of my life. One night, while smoking pot with friends and telling what I thought was a *hilarious* anecdote about being rushed to the ER after lodging a cherry-scented Magic Marker up my nose, I realized I'd always enjoyed sharing potentially amusing stories. So the next morning I decided to officially pursue a career working behind the scenes on a comedy television show. Trying to become an actual writer or performer who might one day share stories *on* one of those shows never occurred to me because I needed a job that was relatively stable—in the event that I'd have to support a family as a single parent one day.

My mother, who raised me on her own in Manhattan after my father died when I was ten months old, always told me, "Wendaaay, after you have kids someday, you can never be financially dependent on your husband. Okay? You guys could get divorced or he could die. And Manhattan private school tuitions are *skyrocketing*. So for the sake of your future children's education, you have no choice but to become a businesswoman, litigator, or dermatologist. And for God's sake, if you want to do something *creative*, it should be kept on the *side*. Like a spicy salad dressing or a fattening mayonnaise." While it wasn't as foolproof as a career in business, litigation, or dermatology, I figured an internship at a comedy show like Letterman or Conan might lead to *some* form of financial security. The internship would probably turn into an entry-level job, and since I would work super-hard, I'd surely climb the ladder and eventually become a successful comedy executive who earned enough money to support children and send them to good private schools.

So I sent a cover letter and résumé to both Letterman and Conan. A few months later I got a call from both of their internship coordinators. I had been accepted for interviews. After going to New York, and meeting with both coordinators, I was offered both internships. I was beside myself. I felt so lucky and honored. But mainly relieved: My future kids would get the private education they needed.

All I had to do was choose which internship to take.

But I am not a decision-making type person. I once remained in the coat section of Bloomingdale's for a solid six hours, debating between five equally unattractive bulbous down jackets. I ended up buying all five, with the intention of taking them home, trying them on for each and every one of my friends, and then returning four. But even after a month, after every pro and con had been weighed, I was still undecided. In my paralysis I was forced to return the entire bunch and I got sick all winter because of my lack of protection against biting winds.

Anyway, I simply didn't have what I considered to be enough information about Letterman or Conan to make a totally informed decision. Letterman's internship program started a day before Conan's, so I figured I'd start at Letterman, see how it was, and *then* decide.

So Monday morning at 10:00 A.M. I showed up at Letterman's offices, put on a cool Letterman ID pin, and introduced myself to the other interns. All day I eagerly faxed and copied and collated. As I left I was told that the executive producer had once been an intern—just what I needed to hear.

Yet I still needed *one* day at Conan—*one day*. So I could properly compare. The education of my future children depended on it.

So Tuesday morning I woke up at 9:00 A.M. and called Letterman's middle-aged internship coordinator. I'm not a liar, really, I've always hated lying, but in this case it was a necessary evil. I went ahead and told her I needed the day off—I was feeling a bit sick. She understood and told me to rest up and feel better. I thanked her and headed straight to Conan's offices to start *their* internship program.

I showed up at Conan's offices at 10:30 A.M., put on a cool Conan ID pin, and introduced myself to the other interns. All day I eagerly faxed and copied and collated. As I left I heard that many of the producers there had once been interns.

This was going to be tough. Conan was definitely a more enjoyable show, but Letterman had been around forever, so perhaps had a better chance of lasting for another decade. But then again there was a very appealing casual nature to Conan's offices, and the staff did seem friendlier. If I ever needed to bring my future children to work, I would totally trust the PAs to look after them for a few hours while I was off doing something important behind the scenes. But then again Letterman's office was nicely carpeted, so maybe it would be more baby-proof. But then again Conan's color copier was rather hi-tech, so maybe they had a superior employee family health plan.

Clearly, I just needed *one* more day at Letterman. So I could *truly* properly compare. And since I had already lied once, really, what would be the harm in lying one more time?

So Wednesday morning I woke up at 9:00 A.M., called Conan's hipster internship coordinator, and told him I needed to take the day off—I was feeling a bit sick. He understood and told me to rest up and feel better. I thanked him, put on my cool Letterman ID, and headed back to Letterman's offices to return to *their* internship program.

Surprisingly, at the end of my second day at Letterman, which was exactly like my first day, I didn't have my answer. Obviously, then, I needed *one* more day at Conan—to really settle it all out. But after nearly a full week of going back and forth, I could barely function. The deception was contaminating my soul. I wasn't eating. I wasn't sleeping. I was out of Klonopin. My boyfriend Amos tried to get me to calm the hell down and just make a goddamn choice already, but I was spiraling into that dark vortex of uncertainty like I'd never spiraled before.

Still, on Thursday morning I somehow managed to make my way back to Conan's offices. I'd forgotten to wake up early to call in sick at Letterman, so I wearily wandered away from the intern station to look for an abandoned cube with a working phone. Instead I snuck into an empty conference room with even more privacy and called Letterman's coordinator.

"Hi Janice. It's Wendy . . . again . . . I know this sounds insane, but, um, I have another conflict."

"Uh-huh."

"I need to see the doctor today. It's the same stomach thing. I don't think I should come in." I lied for, like, the twentieth time.

"Wendy, if you're sick, why are you calling from 30 Rockefeller Plaza, the NBC building?"

This was before the widespread use of caller ID.

"I . . . I am seeing a doctor in midtown, and ran into the building to make a call from their phones?"

"Wendy, you're calling from Conan's offices. I see their extension on my screen here."

I blocked out the rest of the dialogue, but she eventually got me to admit that I was attending Conan's internship at the same time, and fired me. And moments later, Conan's coordinator called me into his office.

"Hey, um, I got a call from the internship coordinator at Letterman. It appears you have been attending both our internship programs. Simultaneously."

"Yeah."

"Well, that is really, really weird. You should probably leave. Like now, I guess?"

The next thing I remember is upchucking in front of the front doors of the building, where the Christmas tree stands in the winter. Not only was I deeply ashamed, and deeply humiliated, but I was sure I'd never be able to have a family because I'd never be able to support them as a single parent.

I started seeing a very schlumpy therapist who wore beaded ankle socks and moccasins. Instead of trying to calm me down, she insisted she could get my internships back! All she would have to do, she said, is call the coordinators and explain that I was suffering from an extreme amount of indecision, which was a symptom of OCD, which was a legitimate disorder under the DSM. They'd *have* to take me back, otherwise it would be discrimination.

While I appreciated the fact that she wanted to remedy the situation, her apparent lack of understanding of the entertainment industry annoyed me more than her beaded ankle socks and moccasins. And she seemed genuinely uninterested in addressing the issues that had caused the severe spiral in the first place. So I stopped seeing her.

Instead, I went on various anxiety medications, officially gave up trying to be behind the scenes, and attempted to just write and perform my potentially amusing stories. Even if it meant sending my future kids to public schools in Brooklyn, where I'd probably want them to go anyway.

Wendy Spero is an actress, comedian, and writer who has performed on NPR, Comedy Central, VH1, NBC, and the Food Network. Her most recent one-woman show, *Who's Your Daddy?* was produced at Edinburgh Fringe Festival after a year-long run at the Upright Citizens Brigade Theatre in NYC. Wendy has been featured in the *New York Post, New York* magazine, *The New Yorker,* and *The New York Times. Back Stage* magazine listed her as one of the Top Ten Standout Stand-ups Worth Watching and she has been named Best Female Comic of the Year by *Time Out New York.* Wendy has contributed to *The New York Times* Op-Ed page, *The New York Times Magazine*'s Funny Pages, *Esquire,* and the best-selling anthology, *Bar Mitzvah Disco.* She recently cowrote a pilot for HBO, and her book *Microthrills: True Stories from a Life of Small Highs* became a *Los Angeles Times* Bestseller.

Sketch Packets

Andrés du Bouchet

No one ever told me I didn't get the job, but I'm pretty sure I didn't since I don't appear to be working there. That pretty much sums up the experience of blindly submitting a comedy-writing packet. For the past ten years I've been writing and performing comedy in New York City with no representation of any kind, just slogging through crappy day jobs while doing comedy at night, and whenever I've sent in a writing submission to Conan, or *SNL*, or anywhere, it's always been the same: You hear nothing, and then later on you still hear nothing, and then much later on you find out who *did* get hired through the comedy grapevine and even *then* you still get a bit of a sinking feeling in your stomach, since as long as you didn't know you didn't get it and you didn't know who did get it, the possibility remained, however slight, that you might get it. But you didn't. And after the weeks or months of gnawing, you finally get that you didn't get it, and you move on. Well, here is some stuff that didn't get me it. But they sure were fun to write. Enjoy!

Late Night With Conan O'Brien Sketch Packet (Spring 2005)
The Guy Who Pretends That He Thinks He's Invisible

A completely naked guy sipping coffee from a mug strolls across the set, waving the mug around and saying in a ghostly voice, "Ooooooh, I am the mysterious free-floating mug of coffee, oooooooh! Beware! I am bold and flavorful and haunted, ooooh!" Disgusted, Conan accuses him of pretending that he thinks he's invisible just so he can expose himself in public. The two engage in a cat-and-mouse game of logic, with Conan trying to prove that the naked guy *knows* he's not invisible, and the naked guy first trying to prove that he really *is* invisible, then trying to prove that he at least *thinks* he is. Finally, the naked guy "realizes" he's not invisible, starts to cover himself as if he's embarrassed, but then proudly struts off with a satisfied grin.

Man with Two Windpipes

This amazing guest was born with two esophagi. During the interview, Conan offers the guest some candy, and the guest starts to choke. Conan is alarmed, but then the guest reveals he was just kidding—"Besides, even if I were choking, I've got two windpipes, so even though one would be blocked, the other one would work, so I'd be fine. Now, let me have some more of that candy." The man has a second piece of candy and starts to choke again. This time Conan laughs it off, but the guest says, "Nope, this time I'm really choking in one esophagus, but that's okay, since my second windpipe is unobstructed, let's just continue the interview." They continue the interview, the guest smiling and answering the questions gamely despite hacking and coughing violently. He casually asks for another piece of candy, and assures Conan he'll be fine. Conan isn't too sure that's a good idea, but gives him the candy anyway. The guest eats the candy, and starts choking even more violently, and looks as if he'll die. Conan panics, but then the guest reveals that he's just joking around again. "Make no mistake, I'm still choking painfully and violently for real in the one windpipe, but the second windpipe is fine, I was just kidding. One more piece of candy, please!" Conan gets so mad that he starts to choke the man, who then reveals, "Go ahead, choke me all you want, I was kidding the entire time about the one windpipe being obstructed at all. You can choke me all night!" After commercial, it's revealed that Conan has assigned an intern to continue choking the guy for the remainder of the show.

Late Night With Conan O'Brien Sketch Packet (Spring 2007)
Hang-Gliding Douchebags

These guys bring a bad attitude to a high altitude! It's Trey and Boner, the Hang-Gliding Douchebags! Two meatheads in hang-gliding gear 'fly' in front of a green-screened panorama, shouting insults at the people offscreen on the ground:

>   TREY
>
> Hey, lady, you're so fat that from up here, you *don't*
> look like an ant!

>   BONER
>
> You just look like a very-far-away fat person!

>   TREY
>
> Hey look, it's Al Roker.

>   BONER
>
> Hey, Al, looks like a 100% chance of showers!
> [spits]

>   TREY
>
> Forecast calls for snow! Woo! [scratches scalp]

>   BONER
>
> Ooh, looks like there's gonna be some funny-
> smelling yellow rain!

>   TREY
>
> (beat) Um. I can't . . . when there's other people
> around.

>   BONER
>
> Oh. Me neither. I've got what do you call it, shy—

>   TREY
>
> Shy kidneys, yeah. Hey, Roker, you lucked out,
> we've got shy kidneys!

TREY

Hey, Roker! F(bleep)k you!

BONER

Go f(bleep)k yourself, Al!

TREY

High five!

TREY and BONER high five, which sends them careening to their deaths on the hillside below. Oddly, their crash culminates with a massive, fiery explosion.

*****

A Ghost, a Snake, and a Bulimic

As Conan announces the following night's guests, he is interrupted by booing, hissing, and gagging sounds. He looks into the audience to see a ghost, snake, and a very skinny woman with a pail. When he scolds them for being rude, they apologize, claiming it's just their nature, since they're a ghost, snake, and bulimic. Conan then continues announcing the following night's guests, and is interrupted by the same sounds again. Except this time, the camera clearly captures that it's the ghost making the gagging noise, the snake booing, and the bulimic hissing. After Conan scolds them again, they feign innocence and promise to be quiet. During Conan's third attempt at announcing the following evening's guests, we hear a cellphone ringing. As it continues ringing, the ghost, snake, and bulimic all sit still, stonefaced. Finally, Conan yells, "Just answer the damn thing!" The snake spits the cellphone into the pail, which the ghost then picks up and answers— "Dude, my friend ate your friend. Boo!" Cut to Joel on his cellphone looking grief-stricken. "Fernando! Mi amor! Nooooo!"

Guitar Solo or Orgasm?

Ladies and gentlemen, this game is simple. We're going to show you a close-up of a person's face, and you have to determine whether that person is playing a guitar solo or having an orgasm.

- Eddie Van Halen's face. He's playing a guitar solo.
- Ron Jeremy's face. He's playing a guitar solo, too! Huh, who would have thought?
- Prince's face. He's doing both. Actually, he's playing one guitar solo and having two orgasms simultaneously.

Friday Night with Greg Giraldo (September 19, 2005)
Monologue Jokes

- A recent study showed that cats can't taste sweets. In other news, dogs can't smell Axe bodyspray for men, and parrots can't see Asians. Just can't see 'em. So if you're an Asian burglar and you've been holding off robbing a place because it's guarded by parrots, go ahead and rob that place.

- I'd like to thank Starbucks for creating a sizing system that allows me to accurately describe my penis as a *Grande*. It's the medium size, you see. No foam. My wife sees to that.

- Every September 11th, I spend the day the exact same way I did on that first terrible day back in 2001. I wake up at noon, turn on CNN, and shit my pants. Then I spend the rest of the day sitting there, crying in my shitty pants. It gets a little harder to muster up the crap and tears each year. This year I had to cry to *Lou Dobbs Tonight.*

- NASA has announced plans to send four astronauts to the moon in 2018. Wow, that's progress. NASA has also announced that by 2035, they hope to perfect the "horseless carriage."

- Federal courts ruled that the Pledge of Allegiance can't be recited in schools because it contains a reference to God. Similarly, I have told my wife she is no longer allowed to talk during sex because of too many references to Gary.

Saturday Night Live Sketch Packet (July 2005)
Tom Cruise's Non-Gay House of Straight Seafood

Int.—a restaurant

A couple dines at a table off to one side. TOM CRUISE enthusiastically bounds out and speaks to the camera.

> ### TOM CRUISE (MYERS)
> Hi, I'm international superstar Tom Cruise, and I'm in love with Katie Holmes, who is a woman! If you're straight like me, you love delicious seafood at reasonable prices, and that's exactly what you'll get at Tom Cruise's Non-Gay House of Straight Seafood!

Two extremely gay male singers come out and bracket TOM, gyrating suggestively as they sing to the tune of Kenny Loggins' "Danger Zone."

> ### SINGERS (FORTE AND RICHARDS)
> Highway to the seafood zone! Highway toooo the seafood zone, yeah! (flirtatiously) Bye Tom, see you later . . .

The singers dance off.

> ### TOM CRUISE
> Those were just some straight friends of mine. Hey, I know that finding delicious seafood at reasonable prices seems like a *Mission: Impossible.* Eating cheap seafood is *Risky Business,* and can often produce (waves away an imaginary fart) *Days of Thunder.* But you'll find only the best seafood here at Tom Cruise's Non-Gay House of Straight Seafood, where we're the *Top Gun* at broiled scallops! Our sushi chefs have got *All The Right Moves,* and our clams casino is *Far and Away* the best.

The singers dance back on.

SINGERS

Highway to the seafood zone! Highway toooo the
seafood zone, yeah!

The singers dance off.

TOM CRUISE

Oh look, here comes one of our straight waiters,
Sapphire, with our *Legend*-ary shrimp *Cocktail*.

SAPPHIRE, a scantily clad waiter in tight short-shorts roller skates in
with a platter of shrimp cocktail. He is even gayer than the singers. He
just keeps dipping one shrimp into the cocktail sauce over and over.

SAPPHIRE (ARMISEN)

Hi, Tom, you look really straight today.

TOM CRUISE

You do, too, Sapphire, and I love Katie Holmes.
What's the weather like tonight?

SAPPHIRE

Looks like it's going to *Rain, Man*.

TOM CRUISE

Jerry Maguire Magnolia.

Awkward beat.

SAPPHIRE

Okay byeee. See you at wrestling practice later.

SAPPHIRE leaves.

TOM CRUISE

I'm getting hard just thinking about it. You straight
guys know what I'm talking about! I'm so excited
I'm *Losin' It*. Um. *Interview with the Vampire*. Anyway,
come on down to Tom Cruise's Non-Gay House of

Straight Seafood, where you'll find seafood so delicious and reasonably priced, I must be straight!

The singers return.

SINGERS

Highway to the seafood zone! Highway toooo the
seafood zone, yeah!

TOM CRUISE

Oh man, yeah, work it, girls . . .

*****

After writing and performing his unique brand of comedy in New York City
for the past ten years, **Andrés du Bouchet** recently lugged a suitcase full of T-
shirts, shorts, and cutlery to Los Angeles to be a staff writer for *Talkshow with
Spike Feresten*. In New York he was best known as the creator and host of *Giant
Tuesday Night of Amazing Inventions and Also There Is a Game*. Andrés has also appeared in sketches on *Late Night with Conan O'Brien*, *Tough Crowd with Colin
Quinn*, and *Cheap Seats*. Du Bouchet's unique monologues, sketches, and ab-
surdist style make him hard to miss, as do his loudness and size.

Jared

Sara Schaefer

It all began with a note dropped on my desk at the end of drama class in the eleventh grade.

It was from Jared. Though shorter than me, and mmmmaybe with a slight mullet, he was my Jordan Catellano, and I was obsessed with him. All the girls were. But he gave *me* the note. It said, in part:

> DEAR SARAH,   9-24-94
>   I LOVE YOU. I'M SORE OF IT. I
> JUST WANT TO BE NEAR YOU, AND WHEN
> I'M SAD I THINK OF KISSING YOU
> AND I SMILE.

So what if he misspelled my name. *He loved me!* Let the making out begin! But wait . . . it goes on:

> I'M NOT GOING TO DO ANYTHING ABOUT
> IT, THOUGH. I KNOW I WOULD EVENTUALLY
> HURT YOU.

Wait . . . what?

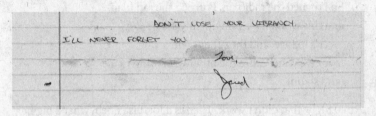

> DON'T LOSE YOUR VIBRANCY.
> I'LL NEVER FORGET YOU
> Love,
> Jared

It's as if he was writing me a goodbye letter—but hello, it was September, the beginning of the school year, and we still had another year before he graduated.

Clearly, Jared needed some persuading. I mean, you can't *love* someone and not go for it, right? *Right?* All the movies and TV shows and books and grown-ups in my life had taught me that the word "love" meant something. If someone said it to me, clearly, we were going to get married, live in a cottage in the English countryside a la *Howards End*, and, of course, be famous.

So, I wrote him a passionate note saying essentially just that and, if I remember correctly, I quoted Sophie B. Hawkins. Then, I got this note in return:

> DEAR SARA,
>   I'M SORRY I TOLD YOU I LOVED
> YOU. IF I HAD KNOWN YOU'D BE ANNOYED,
> I WOULDN'T HAVE TOLD YOU. I THOUGHT
> THE LACK OF A RELATIONSHIP WOULD HURT,
> BUT I THOUGHT I SHOULD BE HONEST.
> I GUESS I LOVE YOU TOO MUCH TO HURT
> YOU. I'M SORRY I HAVE HURT YOU, BUT
> I WANTED YOU TO KNOW HOW I FELT. (FEEL)
>   Love,
>   Jared

Okay, it just wasn't adding up. How could he *love* me and not want to be my boyfriend? I decided I had to do something drastic. So, in between classes, I pulled him into an empty stairwell, and I sang— a cappella—

> So I turned the radio on, I turned the radio up,
> and this woman was singing my song:
> lover's in love, and the other's run away,
> lover is crying 'cause the other won't stay.
> (and so on)

Amazingly, that didn't work. Thanks a lot, Lisa Loeb, what a big help you turned out to be.

What followed was months of notes, frustrating phone calls, rumors, girls running and crying down the hallway—all of us awash in Jared's growing legacy of drama and mystique. Through it all, no matter which girl he was kissing, he maintained that he "loved" me. So I maintained my hope.

It all came to a head in the late summer of 1995. I received a package in the mail—containing a three-page letter and a mix-tape. It was from Jared.

It began like this:

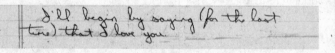

Yeah, you mentioned that, like a hundred times.

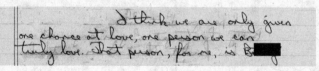

My heart imploded.

I am not going to apologize for my (and our) actions at the Indigo Girls concert.

Okay. They were practically dry humping on the blanket next to mine.

I never meant to hurt you. I did love you.

And that was that. After a twenty-minute sob-fest, I wiped my face and slowly put the mix-tape, labeled SARA—FINAL MIX, into my boom box. The songs that played were nothing short of cruel. Here are some of the songs he put on this "Final" tape:

"It Ain't Me Babe" by Bob Dylan
"The End" by The Doors
"Everybody Hurts" by R.E.M.
"Stay Away" by Nirvana
"Black" by Pearl Jam

The tape came to an end. I sat on my bed, trying to get a breath. This was the day I learned why they call it a crush.

Of course, the pain faded, and over many years, I did my fair share of heart breaking until finding a love that transcended that silly little word. Jared married one of his many high school sweethearts. And no, it wasn't Betty. Last I heard, they divorced.

Sometimes now, when I hear those songs, my heart makes a tiny lurch. Especially with the Pearl Jam song. If it comes on, and I'm in a car alone, I will scream the ending lyrics—so loud I see stars—"I KNOW SOMEDAY YOU'LL HAVE A BEAUTIFUL LIFE, I KNOW YOU'LL BE A STAR... IN SOMEBODY ELSE'S SKY, WHY...

WHY . . . WHYYYYYYY CAN'T IT BE MIIIIIIIIIIINE????" And then I scream, "I MARRIED A SEXY NOVELIST YOU ASSHOLE!"

Jared, if you're out there, I harbor no ill will.

Sara Schaefer writes, performs, and produces comedy in New York City. She was the host of AOL's online music/comedy show, *The DL*, until AOL decided it was too expensive and gave it the boot. She was also a featured performer at the 2007 U.S. Comedy Arts Festival in Aspen. She is currently an editor at bestweekever.tv. Find more at www.saraschaefer.com.

Stephen Colbert *Law & Order* Fan Fiction

Rob Klein

A couple of years ago, I applied to be the Web writer for *The Colbert Report*. I was rejected. Probably with good reason. My submission was this Stephen Colbert fan fiction.

MANHATTAN GOURMET DELI—421 FIRST AVENUE—WEDNESDAY, FEBRUARY 23

"Poor guy," muttered Detective Lennie Briscoe. He finished drawing a chalk outline around the victim, then turned to face his partner, Rey Curtis.

"Wrong place, wrong time," said Curtis, who was handsome. "Looks like all he wanted was a couple Krispy Kremes."

"I guess it's true," mused Briscoe. "They really are bad for your health."

"Wow, Briscoe." The voice belonged to the brash new kid— Stephen Colbert. "That's your joke? 'They really are bad for your health?' Wow." Colbert slowly shook his head in disbelief, then mysteriously made the universal sign for "blow job."

"Take a walk, Colbert. We got this covered."

"Oh?" Colbert casually nodded to the crime scene. "Not what it looks like to me."

Briscoe turned back around to find his crime scene being raided by a pack of drunken dogs. Several had attached themselves to Curtis, who was screaming.

"Geez, Louise," muttered Briscoe.

With a knowing sigh, Colbert bagged the evidence, apprehended three suspects, and enrolled the dogs in a substance-abuse program he had read good things about.

"Don't worry, Briscoe," said Stephen, "I can keep a secret if you can."

As if on cue, Briscoe tripped over the dead body and broke something.

OFFICE OF THE DISTRICT ATTORNEY—1012 THIRD AVENUE—SATURDAY, FEBRUARY 26

"It won't hold up in court! You know that, Stephen!" Colbert was getting a lecture from the female assistant D.A. Not the blonde one—the one before her. The hot one.

"Jack McCoy would have never stood for this!" she exclaimed in a voice both professional and sexual.

Colbert smiled sweetly and stroked her cheek. "I'm not Jack McCoy. I think you know that firsthand."

The lady D.A. could not help smiling, as if at a shared secret. Colbert winked in return, a subtle reminder of the fact that they were boning on the sly.

"She's got a point, Colbert." District Attorney Adam Schiff stood up from his chair. "Facts are facts."

"Adam, Adam, Adam." Colbert playfully tousled the D.A.'s hair, then let his hand linger on the back of the D.A.'s head. "Come on," Colbert whispered. "This is me you're talking to. This is Stephen."

The D.A. lowered his eyes and hoped he was not blushing.

NEW YORK COUNTY CRIMINAL COURT—100 CENTRE STREET—
TUESDAY, MARCH 17

A sense of expectation filled the courtroom. Since taking over as district attorney, Stephen Colbert had won ninety-nine straight convictions. One more and he would be on the Supreme Court.

"Urf! Urf-urf-urf!" Colbert was in the middle of performing a walrus impression, which was in no way related to the case at hand.

"Mr. Colbert!" The judge banged his gavel. "Do I need to hold you in contempt of court?" Unfazed, Stephen repeated the judge's words back to him, but in a funny voice that made it sound like he was gay. The courtroom erupted with laughter. The tall guy from *Criminal Intent* blew an air horn, while the cast of the short-lived *Trial by Jury* spinoff all joined hands and pretended an electrical current was passing through their arms.

"Order!" screamed the judge. "Order! Mr. Colbert, I am appalled! This man stands accused of murder, yet you refuse to take his case seriously!"

"That's because he didn't do it." Colbert looked the judge squarely in the eyes. "You did."

Everyone gasped—even the character played by Ice-T.

"Are you out of your mind?" exclaimed the judge. "You really think I could strangle someone?"

"But your honor . . . I never said that the victim was strangled."

The jury gave Colbert a ten-minute standing ovation before sentencing the judge to death.

Rob Klein is a writer for *Saturday Night Live*. Before that he was an editor of *The Harvard Lampoon* and a member of War Dogs, a sketch comedy group that may have performed upwards of two times.

A Funny Kind of Marxist

Jordan Roter

My agent stopped calling me back. The death rattle that is her voice mail haunts me like the twisted laugh track of my career nightmare. I needed some control. Somebody had to pay. I knew where I had to go: Pottery Barn.

When I first moved into my L.A. apartment about a year ago, "The Barn" kept messing up my drapery order, and I kept complaining. Every time I complained, I got a $50 gift certificate for my trouble. By the end of the drapery debacle, I had racked up $200 worth of gift certificates and a very intimate relationship with my next-door neighbors.

So on one uncharacteristically gloomy L.A. afternoon, I clutched said certificate like a life raft and headed to the Beverly Center. I did not need furniture. I needed cash.

"Oh, you can't do that," my friend Melissa warned me.

Can't-shmant.

I scoured the store for the cheapest thing I could find. I picked out a cheerful, yellow aromatherapy candle; CALM, it said. I was on a mission. See, I've been a little down, folks. This acting thing was getting to me. I was losing my N.Y. edge. In fact, I was afraid I'd already lost it. I imagined all my friends preparing for an intervention in my tiny living room.

The salesperson rang me up. "So I'll just put the remainder on store credit, okay?" "Um, no, actually, I'd like the cash please," I said smugly, but sweetly. I felt like a ventriloquist. I hadn't heard that confidence in my voice in months. "Let me get the manager." Oooo, the manager, I'm shaking in my boots, I thought. I waited. Patiently. My hand was steady.

The manager was a young, harried woman. I was momentarily distracted by the shiny object that hung around her neck: a key. The key to my renewed happiness and confidence hung precariously around the neck of "the manager" at Pottery Barn. "So I'm just going to put the rest of this on store credit," she parroted. Nice try.

"No, I'd like cash please."

She laughed. That's right, I thought, laugh now while you still can.

"I'm sorry, but we cannot give you the cash back for a four-dollar purchase."

"Actually, with tax, the purchase comes to seven dollars and fifty-eight cents and I will happily take the store credit if you can show me where in your 'literature' it states the actual percentage of the store credit one must spend in order to get cash in return."

She was a deer in my headlights. "Do you have a Mission Statement?" I added.

I was getting carried away. Had I gone too far? My headlights were faltering and her vision was being restored. Was I going to fail? Was this going to be the failure that finally put me over the edge? I looked at my hand—still steady, for now. "It is not our policy. . . ." she quavered.

But?

"But, I'll do it for you . . . this once. . . ."

I was back. "I mean, if we did this for everyone," she continued as I nodded, ever sympathetic to the Pottery Barn plight, "we'd go broke."

I worry not for Pottery Barn.

And that was when she laid approximately $192 worth of crisp green currency in my eager little hand. There would be no intervention today. I had restored my own confidence. This town wasn't through with me yet. I felt more inspired than when successful actors and actresses receive awards and say things like, "To all those actors out there with a dream, don't give up!" Well, I stand behind no podium, but from in front of one Pottery Barn counter, for just a moment, I remembered what it was like to not take no for an answer. And I'd like to thank the little people.

Jordan Roter was born and raised in New York City. After graduating from Brown University, she moved to Los Angeles to pursue her dream of being an actress, and subsequently, to get rejected on a daily basis. She then worked in film production and development, and once completely rejected in that field, she finally became accepted in the world of young adult fiction. Jordan is the author of the novels *Girl in Development* and *Camp Rules.* DreamWorks and Montecito have just optioned Jordan's novel, *Camp Rules,* for her to adapt to the big screen. She lives in Los Angeles with her husband.

You Are the Most Obnoxious Person Alive

Peter Hyman

In May of 2004 I wrote a six-hundred-word article for *New York* magazine entitled "The New Cab Calculus," never realizing it would give rise to an international rejection. The piece was a first-person essay pegged to the 25% increase in taxi fares happening that same week. It was a pretty straightforward work of service journalism, laying out the facts of looming fare increase with a touch of colorful set-up ("What other city can boast the gruff cabbie as a mascot? Forty thousand of these lone rangers travel more than a million miles a day . . . We even ride under the inalienable protection of a Taxicab Rider Bill of Rights") and the fiscal mathematics of what the fare increase would mean to a man, such as myself, who took cabs six or so times a week (the answer: about $565 a year). There were also a few personal observations on how all of this would impact my life. Given the nature of writing for a general-interest culture magazine, these were slightly exaggerated for what was intended to be a humorous effect. For example, I suggested that there would be certain situations where I'd no longer rely on the luxury of a cab ride. To wit: "That ten-block round-trip to Circuit City for a new toner cartridge will become an opportunity to walk with the people. And my perfect punctuality record for dinners with married ex-girlfriends? It's likely to slip."

It was a lightweight, modestly funny reported story, with a mix of facts and frivolity. That is to say, it was a magazine article. It came, it went, life continued. So I was surprised when, seven months after publication, I received an email subject-lined, "You are the most obnoxious person alive." The note (reprinted below) went on to detail the ways in which the taxi fare article had offended the young man who sent it. Yet rather than ignore the note or dismiss him as a madman, I took his words to heart. After several days of careful reflection, I decided on a course of action: I would address his concerns (and what it felt like to be rejected) in a nine-slide PowerPoint deck that could be presented to audiences via a '70s-era overhead projector. Obviously. Like the email, that document is presented in the pages that follow. And if "David D." is reading this, I can only hope that his questions are answered, and that he and I can begin to move on with our lives.

From: David <davidd@redacted.com>
Date: Sat, 3 Dec 2005 20:29:18
To: <pdhyman@redacted.com>
Subject: You are the most obnoxious person alive

Hi, you'll have to excuse me if I'm not too clever but I'm a little busy right now, how can you live after writing the things you've written? I stumbled across your piece in *New York Magazine* "The New Cab Calculus", while searching for information on "Ex-New Yorkers." Its funny how I found the exact opposite of the sentiment I was looking for. Here I am, a 22-year-old native, abroad, looking for someplace else to live upon returning to the USA, and what do I find? Some of the most inane drivel Ive ever read, and of course, you: probably the most vapid, insipid writer ever. At first I gave you the benefit of the doubt, everyone writes something shitty, and that story was inanely shitty. Talk about trash. Don't get me wrong, Taxis are cheap in NYC compared to other parts of the world- a taxi from Narita airport will easily run you 4 times that of Kennedy, but its not so much the content so much as it's your tone. This tone of obnoxious entitlement. To actually say *Friends* reflects life in NY, Jesus. Were you being ironic? It's so ridiculous that someone like you would actually utter something like that, and yet, perfectly plausible. Goddamnit. Why are you so obnoxious? PLEASE answer me, PLEASE tell me, I would like to know what events in your life led you to be this way. I want to know for 2 reasons: sheer morbid fascination, and to actively avoid the choices you must have made.

Glad I wrote to you,

David D.

You Are The Most Obnoxious Person Alive

(An Annotation Featuring Words, Bullet Points and A Table of Sorts*)

*originally presented in PowerPoint, via overhead projector

"How can you live after writing the things you've written?"

- A steady supply of O_2
- Food, water, and the fact that most of my blood has been replaced with a blend of space-age polymers and Tequiza[1]
- The knowledge that infinite spin-offs for the CSI™ franchise are being shepherded by CBS

[1] This operation took place in Mexico, at a secret laboratory/cantina that does not accept U.S. medical insurance

"while searching for information on 'Ex-New Yorkers'"

- Using the Internet to search for "information" is, of course, a violation of Geneva Accords
- Ex-New Yorkers ≠ proper noun
- Ex-New Yorkers include J.D. Salinger, Robert Zimmerman, and Martin Luther King

"Its [sic] funny how I found the exact opposite of the sentiment I was looking for"

- No definition of terms: If we don't know what he's looking for, how can we know what the opposite of that is?
- "funny ha-ha" or "funny" as in "I curse the fact that I came across you and your infantile writing, b/c I hate everything you stand for?"
- Ending in preposition < proper English

"a 22-year-old native, abroad, looking for someplace else to live upon returning to the USA"

- 22-year-olds should be concentrating on sleeping with women barely old enough to vote, not looking for homes
- Are any of us really natives of anyplace but our own corporate-run imaginations?
- Returning to the USA may not be advisable, given that Congress has recently passed laws forbidding the growth of facial hair, which is common on men who live "abroad"

"some of the most inane drivel I've ever read"

- How much other drivel has he read? We have no sample group against which to compare
- If only my piece and *Crime and Punishment*, then I'm supposed to write "inane drivel"
- Is he referring only to written drivel or does he mean drivel from any/all other mediums?

"the most vapid and insipid writer <u>ever</u>"

- Survey of entire literary canon = impressive
- Where did he find the time? Perhaps living in € helped.
- Usually making this deduction requires more work:

$$I_v = \frac{(JO + BK + com + blg)P}{R^w}$$

My insipid vapidity is made up of my journalistic output plus my book in addition to some stand-up comedy and a modicum of blogging multiplied by my personality, divided by my relationship with women, including my wife, which help buffer the level of insipidness

---

"To say Friends *reflects life in New York.[2] Jesus. Were you being ironic?"*

Irony = For Pussies.

Friends ➜ Single Life in NYC

<u>As</u>

Airwolf ➜ The life of a helicopter pilot working at the behest of a shadowy govt'l org. while searching for his lost brother.

[2] this refers to a comment made during an interview with "Gothamist"

"Why are you so obnoxious?
PLEASE answer me."

Potential Reasons	True / False
—Raised in culture of privilege by indulgent parents?	☑
—Is contractually obligated by the Talmudic Law?	☑
—Possesses a healthy detachment from delusions of grandeur?	☒
—Finds that chicks really dig it?	☑

Appendix A

People that are ≥ obnoxious than me:

1. Katie Couric

2. Simon Cowell

3. That Ass on His Cell Phone Talking Really Loudly About How Bad the Reception Is on His Cell Phone

4. Mahmoud Ahmadinejad, President of Iran

The presentation is over.

Please enjoy a few moments of peaceful, music-based reflection, brought to you by Mr. Bob Seger.

Peter Hyman is a contributing writer for *RADAR* magazine and a frequent contributor to the *San Francisco Chronicle Book Review*. His writing has appeared in dozens of national publications, including the *New York Times*, the *Wall Street Journal, McSweeney's Internet Tendency,* and Slate.com. He is the author of *The Reluctant Metrosexual: Dispatches from an Almost Hip Life* and is an occasional comedic performer. He lives in Brooklyn with his wife and his dog, a chocolate lab named Sophie.

Regarding Our Last-Minute Decision to Pull Vladimir Putin from the 2006 *Sexiest Man Alive* Issue

Ellie Kemper

> I submitted this piece to *McSweeney's* right around the time of the Alexander Litvinenko poisoning. If you remember, Russian President Vladimir Putin was suspected of being one of the evil forces behind this murder. Perhaps he was behind it. Perhaps he still is behind it. The world may never know. Just be wary if Putin ever offers you a taste of his borscht. The news moves fast, and so too must we. Unfortunately, I did not move fast enough, and a different Putin poisoning piece had already been accepted by *McSweeney's*. I guess the lesson here is that one should never underestimate the importance of timeliness. It is next to godliness. Or, it's just worth it to write a timely piece while it is still timely.

To Our Readers:

There has been considerable buzz surrounding our recent decision to remove Russian President Vladimir Putin from our annual list of the sexiest men who are alive. Some readers object, claiming that we are jumping to conclusions. Others support our decision wholeheartedly, agreeing that it is entirely appropriate.

We stand by our decision, and we think that we are right.

A Sexy Man is composed of many things. First and foremost, he is composed of sexiness. Of course, sexiness is not something that can be measured in pints or pounds. Sexiness is a quality that transcends measurement. It is like trying to eat a rainbow with a fork. Can you do this? Probably not. Such is the useless attempt to quantify sexiness.

This is what makes our task so difficult.

A Sexy Man might have dreamy eyes, bushy eyebrows, a strong jawline, almond-shaped lips, or a broad forehead. His sexiness might be in the way he walks, or how he darts his eyes, or how only the right side of his mouth turns up when he smiles. He might have strong pectoral muscles. All of these things are sexy, and all of these things contribute to the overall impression of sexiness.

However.

A Sexy Man would never be implicated in the fatal poisoning of a dissident spy. We cannot stress this point enough. Herein lies the distinction between a man who is sexy, and a man who is not.

While it is true that *People* magazine does not have conclusive evidence to confirm that Vladimir Putin is, in fact, responsible for the death of exiled former Russian spy Alexander Litvinenko, it is also true that *People* magazine is not blind. The ferocious denial of the Kremlin that it had anything to do with the spy's death only makes us more suspicious. A person or government does not get so worked up about something unless he or it is actually guilty. Think about how you might have taken the last Nutter Butter, for example, but then energetically insist that it was not you.

It is the same thing.

Vladimir Putin has every reason to have wanted this guy gone. Litvinenko was an outspoken critic of Putin, the Kremlin, and—in his final days—sushi. While *People* magazine does not normally seek to involve itself in international politics, we feel strongly enough about this matter to make our voice heard.

Some of our readers argue that if Putin *is* guilty, then this makes him even sexier. "What could be sexier than a real-life spy thriller?" they point out. We understand their idea, and we agree that spies are sexy. However, Putin is not the spy in this real-life spy thriller. He is the *villain* (maybe).

People magazine does not support the notion that villains are sexy.

Vladimir Putin was a prime candidate for our *Sexiest Man Alive* issue, and was all set to go opposite Patrick Dempsey. Putin has a smile that is coy, a laugh that is rarely heard, and a set of misty eyes to die for. He looks like he always knows a secret, but is keeping it from you. He has a very sexy accent. Putin was very much there in the final mock-up.

But then news of Litvinenko's poisoning broke, and we were forced to reconsider our stance.

Do not mistake us. We certainly hope that Vladimir Putin is not behind this deed, and that the poisoning was merely another case of some bad raw fish. We would love to be reassured that human beings do not poison one another, no matter what mean things one person has said about another. We long for the news that Vladimir Putin is an innocent man.

We fear that this news will never come, though. Humans are inherently evil beings. We, of all periodicals, understand this. At *People* magazine, we are experts on people.

And we smell a rat. A Russian rat.

We encourage you to buy our issue nonetheless, as there are plenty of other Sexy Men in there. George Clooney, Johnny Depp, Enrique Murciano. However, you will not find Vladimir V. Putin among them. Because poisoning is never, ever sexy—even if it is done with as obscure and exotic a poison as Polonium-210.

Also, remember how he kissed that little boy on his naked stomach once? Not sexy.

As always, we remain devoted to the cause of People everywhere.
—The Editors of *People* Magazine
E *Pluribus People*

Ellie Kemper is an actress in New York City. She has a one-woman stage show, *Dumb Girls*, which she is constantly trying to make into a many, many multi-million-dollar film deal. Ellie is a contributing writer for *The Onion*, and has also written for *McSweeney's Internet Tendency*.

Spill of Heaven, Aisle Seven

Luis Amate Perez

I used to search Craigslist every day for acting gigs and writing jobs. One day I came across an ad that said something like, "Would you like to get paid to edit erotica?"

"Yes, I would."

So I responded to the ad, and a couple weeks later they got back to me. They wanted to see an example of my work. I had never written erotica before, so "Spill of Heaven, Aisle Seven" was my very first attempt at it. Apparently, they liked it and called me in for an interview—a real interview, in a real office building, in a real Financial District of Manhattan. I landed the job and for three months I wrote and edited erotica on a daily basis (eight hours in a cubicle, with an hour break for lunch).

However, "Spill . . ." had never been published, so when classmates of mine at City College were putting together their second issue of the literary [sic] journal, and I was asked to submit something, I sent them my very first pages of smut. The editorial staff was obviously not turned on.

Clean Up, Aisle Nine shot through my ears like a phonic act of God. At first I thought it must have been because I was idling, waiting for Loquacious to pass the customer's items over the scanner; waiting for her dark plump fingers to grip the Very Thin Sliced Wheat Bread from Pepperidge Farm; waiting for her lavender-pink-tipped fingernails to dig into the cardboard skin of the Honey Bunches of Oats; waiting for her to touch something else—anything else—just so I could bag it.

We were all out of paper bags—I had checked the stockroom. I had been in Bunnies for at least three hours, having run in right after school. And I wasn't idling; it was my job to help Loquacious pack the customers' groceries—well, at least the most pleasurable job I had to do around the supermarket. I hated mopping up accidents. But luckily the call over the loudspeaker had come when it did; another minute staring at the outline of Loquacious's left breast, as it strained to escape her tight, white, short-sleeve, button-down shirt and Bunnies-issued green smock, and I would have been really embarrassed. The next day I would probably have had to add another layer of underwear to my standard two.

"That's you," Loquacious said.

"Excuse me?" The pale customer piled more groceries onto the conveyer belt.

"I ain't talkin' to you. I'm talking to him."

I looked at the customer and smiled, but I was mostly smiling to myself. Loquacious wasn't looking at me, but she *was* talking to me.

"That it?" Loquacious said, ending in a huff and a puff, just before the woman piled another three boxes of Honey Bunches of Oats onto the conveyor belt.

Aisle 9

Lightbulbs	Juice
Housewares	Eggs
Yogurt	Biscuits
Milk Products	Butter

It was the worst spill I had ever seen in Bunnies: Gold's Prepared Horseradish with Beets and Vita Herring in Sour Cream. In my two months working there I had never seen a customer purchase either of these provisions—and I would have seen them do it, too, because I would have packed them—at least if it happened on my shift. But even if it did happen, and I wasn't there, I would have had to restock the shelf—and this specific restocking had never happened.

On the shelf, the jars looked like goofy novelties—a joke, the thought of which was meant to turn your stomach. On the floor, under the cold fluorescent-blue lights, they were just *sick*. The two ailments mishmashed, breeding a smell that could cut you worse than any glass shard drowning in the goop. I kept my distance.

In the locker room I was finally able to breathe through my nose. I was on my way to get the mop and bucket when I stopped at Loquacious's locker—I had to. It was unlocked. *She trusts me*, I thought. I opened it slowly, as I had done on only two other occasions, and the smell of the cocoa butter and the vitamin-E-enriched lotion she used on her hands and elbows swept over my face. Her navy-blue Knicks sweater hung there like a queen's garment. I held myself back from trying it on again—I had only done that once. And at the time it was so big on me I felt the way my five-year-old sister must have felt when she tried on my father's Queen's College sweater, the one he used to wear all the time before he lost fifty pounds on the Atkins diet. The Knicks sweater felt so good on my body, like an extra blanket on a winter's night when my mother forgets to turn up the heat in the house. Ever since that *one* time I donned her sweater, I'd been trying to bulk up, eat more, do push-ups every day to build my chest, and hopefully take away from my condition. "Why's your chest have a dent in it?" the guys in seventh grade used to ask me, and I'd have to tell them, "It's called *pectus excavatum*. I'm normal. So shut up."

I closed the locker, and dropped down to the floor. By the fifth push-up I was thinking about the cornrows on Loquacious's head. They were perfect. I wondered what they would feel like. *If I asked her, would she let me touch them? Stroke them?*

I lost count of the push-ups when my glasses started to fog up, so I got up from the floor and sat on the bench. I wiped the lenses with the handkerchief I kept in my back pocket.

And here you might want to wipe your glasses, too, because when I look up, and the glasses are back on my face, she's there. She's leaning against the wall, just below the Boar's Head sign. I swallow the saliva that's pooled on my tongue.

She walks over to me, reaches out her hand to meet mine, and pulls me up to eye level. When I think she's going to speak, she turns away and pulls me out into the supermarket. *People are going to see us.* She doesn't care, but I do. She takes off my glasses and tosses them over her shoulder. Everyone disappears. I'm afraid I won't be able to see her—I'm afraid she'll be blurry—but then my vision comes back. There she is leading me down Aisle 9, and the Gold's Prepared Horse-Radish with Beets and the Vita Herring in Sour Cream are back on their shelf. She leads me down another aisle and another and another—we travel the whole distance of Bunnies. She doesn't say a word. She just stops at Aisle 7, and turns to me.

I'm embarrassed to kiss her, but she makes it all right for me to open my mouth. Her painted nails glint, and I shut my eyes. When I open them, she's holding my braces in her hand. I run my tongue over my smooth teeth, straightened a year and a half prematurely. She leans in—or is already there—and massages my teeth with *her* tongue, starting with the eyetooth that was once lodged too high up in my gum. It feels like my own tongue is taking another lap around my mouth, but it's hers. It's all Loquacious.

Killian's Irish Red and Yuengling Original Black & Tan surround us. My chest is exposed, ripped with oiled muscle. She is so light on top of me, dry humping me into rock-hard form. I squeeze on her giant coal-colored breast, and suck at the nipple in the middle of her even-darker areola. Chocolate. *You taste like chocolate.*

She pulls my penis out—no, my *cock*—and she's taken aback. Breathless. I look at her as if asking, *is something wrong*, but knowing that something is right, very right. She opens her mouth, and gasps the words, *SO BIG*, before she takes all 15, 18, 1,000 inches into her mouth.

Her vagina—no, *pussy*—is bubbling over her thick, curly muff, like the Schweppes Club Soda foaming on the shelves now. She needs me inside her. I agree. *Yes, that sounds like a good idea.* She jumps onto my cock and rides it up and down like a horsy on a merry-go-round—but beautiful. Instead of the calliope, all I hear is her singing, *too big, too big, too big.*

I reach up and grab her by the cornrows, and like a bottle rocket it ignites her and it shoots her up into the sky with a long stream of semen—*cum*—trailing behind her butt. And I continue to burst into the air like a roman candle. The whole place is going up in flames now, even though it really wasn't fire coming out of me.

But Loquacious doesn't let me get the apology out, because when she comes down she lands hard and heavy on my face, smothering me between her labia, making me drink her hazel juices. *Chocolate. Everything in you is chocolate.*

"What the fuck you doin'!" a voice suddenly screamed out in front of me.

I froze, regained my breath, and realized where I was:

My pants and two pairs of underwear—wrapped around my ankles.

The damp hood of the Knicks sweater—a basket for my penis and testicles.

My chest bare—still sunken.

Loquacious—looking right at me. For the first time.

Luis Amate Perez is an M.F.A. Creative Writing student at The City College of New York. He has been published in the literary magazine *Fiction*. In addition to his fiction and poetry, Luis both writes and performs for stage, film, and television, often credited as Lou Perez. He has his B.A. from the Gallatin School of Individualized Study at NYU.

Rejections from *The Onion*

Janet Ginsburg

At *The Onion*, the need for new material is constant. The pace at which writers produce material is staggering, and it never, ever stops. Invariably, there's a good deal of rejection involved—most people just learn to take it in stride.

Some people don't. Some people—like, oh, maybe, ME, occasionally find that they spend more time poring over rejected jokes (headlines) than they actually spent writing them in the first place, which might be part of the problem.

Lots of times I'll find myself up very, very late at night—particularly if I have some sort of looming deadline—examining and re-examining rejected efforts like the forensics guy on a crime show, trying to figure out exactly what killed the joke—what went wrong, where, when, why, and how. Here's an autopsy on a few jokes that didn't make it.

> No One Can Tell Mime's Box from His Fish Tank
> Frustrations Quietly Voiced to Bowl of Soup
> Six-Fingered Broker a Dynamo on the Floor

These make me laugh, but they're too quiet. You have to picture them before you laugh—and if you have to do anything before you laugh at a joke, it's too late. Plus, the broker joke is awful.

> Hurricane Katrina Expected to Break Up Around Paul Prudhomme

I like this. It was topical, and Paul Prudhomme is fat.

Sometimes, I was obviously just writing when I was hungry:

Grandma Stockpiling Almond Roca

Sloppy Joe Made with Indifference

Taco Bell to Give Away Copies of 'New Tostadament' to Faithful
    Customers

Bunsen Burner Covered in Butter Sauce

The New Tostadament? If I had a sense of shame, it would be surging right now.

Giant Afro Mistaken for Thought Bubble.

I don't know, I think this one is good. It's not funny, though. It's more like . . . "Wow, man." It's like stoner humor.

There were several rightfully rejected jokes about schnauzers:

(Op/Ed) Only a Greenhorn Puts a Schnauzer on the Witness Stand

Schnauzer to Undergo Rhinoplasty

Bears:

Bear's Agent Has Long List of Demands

Bear Who Should Be Hibernating Still Up Watching Leno

Mallomars. Furbys. Chewbacca. And for some reason, miners:

Miner Giving Everybody Coal Again This Christmas

Alcohol, Illegal Drugs Frequently Sold to Miners

I should mention that miners are not generally, implicitly regarded as funny.

Celebrities weren't off-limits:

Nicole Kidman Incapable of Defrosting Anything

Get it?? Because she's *cold!* She's icy cold!

Sometimes, I submitted things that weren't actually jokes:

Man Addressed in Tone of Voice Usually Reserved for Cat

Hearts Drawn All Over Postal Service Exam

Man Sighs, Puts on Pants, Trudges to Liquor Store

Really, those are just sentences. Then there's this one:

(Op/Ed) If I Really Put My Mind to It, I Can Visualize Myself
    Repeatedly Stamping You on the Forehead with a Cookie Cutter

This one:

Girl Would Be Cute If She Had Some Nostrils

And, um—these:

Barky Dog Just Going Bark, Bark, Bark, Bark
Cat Stuck to Face
Melting Grand Marshal Reveals Metal Endoskeleton, Ruining
    Parade

And once in a great while, I still think some of them are funny:

Very Little Ground Broken on World's Tiniest Building
Mexican Government Aims for Achievable Gooooaaaaals in 2007
Lone Man Stranded on Roof Having Trouble Spelling Something
    with Body

No matter what you people say.

Janet Ginsburg has worked as a field producer for *The Daily Show with Jon Stewart*, and was a staff writer at *The Onion*. She has written for publications including *VIBE, Blender, Maxim,* and *LA Weekly*, produced programs for the Discovery, Sci-Fi, and E! Entertainment Networks, and is a co-author of *The Dangerous Book for Dogs*. She lives in New York. www.janetginsburg.com

Worst Man

Todd Levin

This story is approximately ten years old but I only recently committed it to writing, to read at a live show that I knew was going to be attended by my friend, Simon—the subject of the story. I guess I thought it would be fun to re-live the incident together, with some hindsight, or at the very least watch him squirm one more time.

An editor at *The New York Times Magazine,* who also performed at the show that evening, enjoyed this story and asked if I'd be interested in submitting it to the magazine. It went through a series of edits until we were both very happy and excited with the piece, at which point it was reviewed by a more senior editor and rejected without comment. Even though the silent rejection—the worst kind, in my experience— knocked the wind out of me, the editing process resulted in a story that was more honest and more satisfying. So I've got that going for me, right? Right?

My friends, Simon and Jennifer, did not want a traditional wedding. As a young and progressive couple living in a young and progressive Chicago neighborhood, amongst their young and progressive graduate school peers, it was not only Simon and Jennifer's privilege to flaunt the customs associated with matrimony; it was their imperative.

And they went to town, purposefully seizing upon centuries-old traditions and burning them to the ground, the way Chicago itself has the habit of burning to the ground. Surnames were not adopted but, instead, remained separate and autonomous. Let the next generation sort it out! Wedding vows were ridiculed, then discarded. The ceremony would be godless. Bouquets would be greedily clutched, rather than tossed into a pit of less romantically fortunate women—and the bouquets would be made of angry bees. Rather than tossed, rice was cooked, and eaten, or tossed out of ironic spite. Wedding cake was replaced with a giant soap carving of The Jedi Council, surrounded by piles of loose change for a nearby vending machine.

Their dedication to the avant-garde extended all the way to the bachelor party. As the Best Man—or, more appropriately, "The Especially Thoughtful But In No Way Unfairly Superlative Gender-Neutral Confederate"—it was my responsibility to plan this function. Simon delivered a clear message to me regarding the party. There would be no pornographic material, no naked playing cards or spoken innuendo or baked goods formed into titillating shapes, and definitely no strippers.

Additionally, the party would not be gender-restricted, but would be open to all friends and relatives, from both sides of the marriage. Technically, it wasn't really a bachelor party at all; it was more like a low-key "hoopla."

In one sense, I was grateful to be absolved of stripper-wrangling duties for the hoopla, since I had no experience at negotiating that type of service, and certainly wouldn't know where to start. There is nothing like a consumer reports guide for exotic dancers or an FAQ, so it's difficult to weed out the sordid, crooked entertainers from the truly class acts. And the pay scale for this type of service seems mysterious. Is it an hourly wage, or by volume of clothing removed? Are you expected to provide a hot meal? Bathrobes? Antibiotics? It was an overwhelming number of questions I was happy to never answer.

However, there was an *insistence* in Simon's request that felt a little righteous. And, really, a party without entertainment had no right calling itself a hoopla. But if not a live sex act between two women from broken homes, what kind of entertainment would be equally suitable for an audience comprised of groups of Ph.D. candidates, underage cousins, and old high school friends all meeting each other for the first time?

If you didn't guess "party clown," it's only because you are a reasonable person, unlike me. It turns out it is much easier to hire a clown than it is a stripper. The Chicago Yellow Pages alone contains no less than twenty listings for party clowns. Clowns with names like Patches and Wizz and Yogo and Darnit D competed for my attention with quarter-page ads and inexpertly designed Web sites. There were even specialty acts, like Olé, the Spanish-speaking clown, and one clown billing himself as ApesGrapes, the Midget Clown, whom I suspect was a midget.

I learned the various shades of the clown trade, including the breakdown of clown specialties—magic, slapstick, vaudeville, mime, crowd work—as well as the difference between white-face clowns (often considered the smartest of all clowns), character clowns (which include Red Skelton, Charlie Chaplin, and, by many accounts, Lucy Ricardo), and grotesques (such as Robin Williams). I also learned that, out of some unspoken professional courtesy, no two clowns are permitted to have precisely the same makeup and costume. It's a way of protecting intellectual property.

Then I quickly weeded out clowns based on names, skills, and, in one case, ethnicity. With proper respect to the party guests, I didn't want to retain a clown who would require the room's collective and undivided attention for a forty-five-minute clowning extravaganza. Instead, I tried to find a clown who listed "walk-around show" among his services. A walk-around clown does just that; the clown walks around a room, performing for just a few people at a time, and ultimately providing entertainment in the sum of his feats, rather than their intensity. I think anyone would agree, it's a very spiritual approach to clowning.

I finally settled on a clown named Checkers. He was a character clown of the hobo variety, which I found appropriately poignant, so we went over the details of the hoopla together. With the exception of one or two children, I told Checkers, the hoopla's guests will be exclusively adult-sized, and many of those adults would be graduate students, specializing in very esoteric fields.

Checkers was unfazed. The hoopla will not begin until after dark, I said, and there will be alcohol. Checkers remained unfazed. He had just the attitude I was looking for in a clown. I put him on my payroll and, in what seemed to me at the time a stroke of eccentric genius but, in retrospect, was clearly an immature act from an immature man, I vowed to tell no one of my decision to hire a clown for my best friend's bachelor hoopla.

On the evening of the hoopla, I attended a rehearsal dinner with Simon, Jen, their immediate families, and a handful of close friends. Across town, another friend of the couple was preparing his apartment for the hoopla—laying out trays of crudités and imported cheeses Simon and I had purchased earlier that day. Dinner ran long and all of the wine washed any thoughts of Checkers out of my mind.

When the dinner party finally arrived at the hoopla, more than an hour late and happily intoxicated, we were warmly greeted with cheers from everyone within sight. Then, as the cheers trailed off, someone asked, in a very sobering way, "What's up with the f–ing clown?" I guessed they were talking about Checkers.

As best as I've been able to piece together since the evening from various testimonials, Checkers had arrived forty-five minutes before us, just as hoopla guests were beginning to trickle in. Checkers showed up in plainclothes, because the event was being hosted at an apartment in a notoriously unsavory Chicago neighborhood, and Checkers had the good foresight to know that oversized, comically squeaking clown shoes are a tremendous liability in the event that one has to flee from roving gangs of Hispanic murderers. I was told he arrived carrying a guitar case, doctor's bag, and duffel, introduced himself sweetly as John, then asked to be pointed toward a restroom so he could change (i.e., "clown up"). John disappeared into the bathroom with all his belongings and, after fifteen minutes during which a line had started to form, the bathroom door swung open and Checkers emerged with a loud "SURPRIIIIIISE!" and the honking of horns. His baggy pants were stuffed with balloons.

In the forty-five minutes since his grand entrance, Checkers had already bewildered or alienated most of the hoopla guests, without actually entertaining any of them. It's hard to overstate exactly how tremendously negative this clown's impact was on the party. People hated him, on principle—even the children. When I first saw Checkers, he was chasing a ten-year-old girl around the apartment, pleading with her to take the balloon horse he'd just twisted in her honor.

Checkers could not catch a break, and the harder he worked to create joy, the more tension he produced. Sensing the clown's approach, people would form tight circles and turn their backs to Checkers defensively, like a wagon train under attack. I heard at least one person tell Checkers to "please go—just *go!*" Undaunted, he just moved on to the next group of people with his multicolored scarves, magic coins, and hobo resolve.

After a grueling thirty minutes of this, Simon finally approached me, and asked if we could speak in confidence. Through clenched teeth, he kindly explained that maybe it would be a good idea to send Checkers home early. And that's when Checkers sneaked up behind Simon, pulled a large plastic mallet from his waistband, and smashed it on top of Simon's head. It made a bonking sound, and also a loud squeaking sound, like a dog's chew toy.

"Hey, is this the groom? Someone told me you had a thick head!" Checkers announced to the room, to great, disapproving silence. Simon tried to muster a smile.

"Todd," Simon said. "I hope you—*bonk!*—I hope you under—*bonk!*—stand. I hope you understand." *Bonk! Bonk! Bonk! Bonk!* And then Simon was off.

I asked Checkers to meet me in the kitchen.

I'd never fired a clown before, and Checkers didn't make it easy for me. He was bouncing around the kitchen, borderline manic. I tried to get his attention, but he was busy removing from his guitar case a tiny ukelele, which he then began playing with tons of energy, as he walked me through a surefire routine he called "Aloha-ha." I asked Checkers to please put down his ukelele and explained to him that he was doing a magnificent job, but this was, unfortunately, just not a clown crowd. I paid him for his time, adding a very generous tip, and shoved the wad of bills into his fingerless-gloved hand.

Checkers' expression drooped a little, but he was a gentleman, even though he knew he was being sent out into the dark Chicago night in full clown makeup, where he would likely be attacked and stripped of his money and balloons. He returned his ukelele to its out-sized guitar case and squeaked out of the kitchen. As he reached the front door, he turned to wave goodbye and I saw a withering smile beneath his make-up frown. Tonight he was going home, a clown who was both sad on the outside and inside.

Todd Levin is a writer and a comedian. His writing has appeared in *Esquire, Salon, McSweeney's Internet Tendency, The Morning News, RADAR,* and *The Onion,* and he is a contributing writer for the book *The Gawker Guide to Conquering All Media.* When online, he lives at toddlevin.com.

What Makes People Laugh?

Carl Arnheiter and Jon Stewart

"What makes people laugh?" It was one of the more naïve questions I've asked, but it came out of curiosity. Whatever the intention though, I didn't realize it wasn't something that could be tangibly answered.

I was freelancing for a people-focused publication, let's just call it *Person Magazine*, a title whose articles always include a formulaic line—"[Subject's name]'s mom, Frieda, 42, a schoolteacher, and father, Lance, a former stockbroker turned fishing pro, live in Truth or Consequences, New Mexico . . ."—for "context." I had profiled a number of celebrities for them, all with one common denominator—I had no interest in them, their work, or what they had to say about anything. In addition, my editor would want the same story that every publication eventually ran with, resulting in pretty standard interviews with bored subjects. In the end, the stories weren't about what the subject does, but about what they did, making them passive and lifeless.

One of my favorite shows, then as now, was *The Daily Show with Jon Stewart,* and Jon was closing out his first year as host of the show with an hour-long Millennium Special. I pitched a story involving Jon, and my editor replied with two "very important" questions for him to answer:

When are you getting married?
How does it feel to make the salary you're making?

Comedians, if you have the opportunity, are uniformly amazing to speak with. They're engaging, animated storytellers, with a keen eye for detail and an immense amount of intelligence. They can connect two distinct topics with a singular point of view. And asking Jon about his salary—nobody's business but his own anyway—is really a waste of everyone's time.

I dropped by *The Daily Show* set on December 12, 1999, and the place was still buzzing from Bob Dole's appearance the night before. We covered the Millennium Special, and I asked the one question I thought every comedian could answer, "What makes people laugh?"

After a long pause, Jon said, slowly, "Poop? Fake walking into doors? It's sad you've asked me a question I should know the answer to but don't. I'm in a business where I tell a joke at the 8 o'clock show and it kills, and the same joke, different crowd at the 10 o'clock show, nothing. I have no idea what makes people laugh, it's so subjective . . ."

It was fascinating, how could he not know? The piece I wrote was titled "Makes People Laugh." It had substance and insight, two attributes that instantly doomed it with *Person Magazine*.

From the transcript:

I was talking with Kurt Vonnegut for a piece and he told me that creating a joke for him was like building a mousetrap.

Jon Stewart: Let me call Kurt and find out, because that sounds absolutely ridiculous. He said it was like building a mousetrap? He's probably been living in his New York apartment for too long, that's why. It's like killing roaches, don't you understand?

I'm not sure what that means?

Well, what's your take on building a joke, how does it start for you?

Jon Stewart: It's 99% perspiration and 1% love and all that. I can't quantify that, it's an intuition, I mean you learn it, there are techniques. Sometimes they're inspired and they come up from the ether and sometimes it literally is A + B = C, you just throw in a different ridiculous reference. There are formulas, but there's also inspiration, and sometimes we're tapped out, we're throwing formulas out there, but sometimes we're doing it right. And when you're doing it right, it's just natural—it's unexpected, like where you can't—the best jokes are like, "Wow, how'd they think of that?" and the worst are the ones where they go, "Right, David Hasselhoff, I knew that." People say they saw it coming from a mile away.

How'd you learn it?

Jon Stewart: I went to the Institute in France, a small village in France, senior year abroad, from the mayor of Funnytown, Funnytown in France, he taught me, I studied with him for a year, then Soupy Sales and I . . .

I don't know, I think it's just one of those things you learn from doing it, and you know, the funny thing is even though I know how to do it in that yeoman sort of way, there is no "oh now I got it and so it now pours out." But it still takes as much effort and all that, I can do it a little quicker than I used to be able to, but the great stuff still comes in the same percentage that it ever came. There are some guys whose "in the clouds" shit is tremendous, but for the rest of us, we're pounding it out in that manner.

What about the notion that comedians are bitter people?

Jon Stewart: Well then you've never been a part of the Funnybones group hug.

I mean, do you find you have a particular ax to grind?

Jon Stewart: I don't know, I found the bitterness factor a lot higher at the bar I used to work at in Trenton. From my experience, a lot of the guys and women that I've met are some of the smartest, nicest people. Yeah, you know, happy is such a relative term, but I've definitely heard that, that comedians are born of pain and what kind of clown are you, the cryin' on the inside kind. No, I know a lot of people outside the business who are miserable too.

I think life is hard, and that's what happens. You get let out of school and it's "I gotta work for seventy fucking years, are you kidding me?"

But my experience with comedians hasn't been that they are any—you know, show business in general is somewhat filled with hubris and psychosis, I've seen that, but that's also in Los Angeles, it's like, go to Vegas, that's filled with the same single-minded psychosis that Los Angeles is.

Are you as comfortable as an actor as well?

Jon Stewart: Oh, absolutely, again, training at the Institute. No, no, I'm comfortable when they let me be exactly who I am, I can do that sort of, but no, I'm not comfortable as, like if they gave me a character and I had to encompass and inhabit, I don't even know what those words mean. When actors talk to me I sometimes literally glaze over because I have no idea what they're talking about in terms of "I feel the sadness of my youth and I used that." Basically, I go, "Did I look angry in that? Yeah, I think so. All right."

So *Playing by Heart*, a strange experience?

Jon Stewart: It was strange. I think the thing that helped me most for that was interviewing people, because you've got the idea of "Oh right, you say something and I listen to you, then I say something back." But, yeah, it was more weird because you're meeting all these people—I met James Bond, you know, that was pretty psychotic. But they all had the dramatic stuff, love and dying, and I just had to come in and crack a couple jokes and look at a dog's balls and get out of the movie, so it wasn't so bad.

I started performing improv comedy shortly after the interview with Jon, and our conversation kept coming back to me. Talking with comedians about their work seemed like a great way to learn about making people laugh. And now that I was onstage, these conversations could take place there, too.

I created *Inside Joke*, a show where just that sort of thing happens. I've never seen *Inside the Actors Studio*, so I have no idea if they're similar, but I've read a few times that there's a lot less James Lipton in my show. I find this helpful in distinguishing the two.

Since the first show with Lewis Black in late 2001, I have had the privilege of sharing the stage with an amazing cast of comedians, writers, and actors, each and every one of them with an impressive, enviable body of work to their credit.

The show has taught me more than I had ever hoped, not only about comedy, but even about how certain foods flavor certain bodily fluids. I have no idea where we'll wind up before we say goodnight. And in what other forum would I be able to challenge actor Steve Guttenberg to a crying contest?

And after all the research that goes into them, all the scheduling and phone calls and email, I'm reminded of why I do this with the first laugh of every show. Making the audience laugh is a true gift. Making a roomful of people laugh with/at you because of something you've said or done is a feeling I hope everyone can experience.

From the start, I should have realized "What Makes People Laugh?" was something that would never have made the pages of *Person Magazine*. But it being killed was the best possible outcome as it allowed me to answer the question without ever having to ask it again.

Carl Arnheiter is a writer, comedian, and former "musician" living in New York, and the creator and host of *Inside Joke* (inside-joke.com) at the Upright Citizens Brigade Theatre.

Universal Disdain, Hoffnung einer Frau

Annabelle Gurwitch

In the early 1980s, my life dream was to act in expressionistic German dramas in unheated basements, Off-Off-nowhere-near-Broadway where you had a reasonably good chance of sleeping with the entire cast.

It turns out that this goal is not hard to achieve, but, as they say, be careful what you wish for.

My introduction to this scene came on my campus visit to NYU where I was hoping to gain admittance and study theater. Following my audition with the head of the department, I was given the address of a production being staged by their students in one of their theater departments known as The Experimental Theatre Wing. I was told I might want to check it out.

There was no set, no lighting to speak of, no costumes, no script, no delineation between the cast and the audience. The two cast members were attired in ripped '80s-era punk clothing and they themselves appeared to be somewhat unkempt. The two floated between the audience and the "performance area," which was simply a corner of the room where the audience wasn't sitting. The actors were clearly improvising, they were speaking at the very same time and they cursed! In the middle of the play, one of them jumped on top of a piano, sang a self-composed song of disaffection, began gyrating and yelling, "I'm fucking a piano," after which a pizza delivery guy showed up with real pizzas in the middle of the show, which they ate and shared with the audience.

I myself had been acting since I could speak in community theater productions at Temple Beth Shalom in Miami Beach and had never experienced anything that resembled this production. Our drama teacher had understandably bypassed the Brechtian alienation effect in our lessons. The parents of the children at Temple Beth Shalom didn't want to hear their children intone the discordant tunes from *Mahagonny* extolling the decadence of life in a boomtown in Alaska. They wanted to enjoy their well-groomed kids singing catchy show tunes from *Fiddler on the Roof* about being exiled from a shtetl in Eastern Europe. The ETW staging seemed degenerate, vaguely political, and possibly unhygienic. I can still remember thinking, I have no idea what they're doing, but I want to do *that*.

I began studying at ETW that fall and immersed myself in pot-smoking and learning to give my fellow actors massages. Both were encouraged by the faculty and apparently two of the most important skills needed to do this type of acting.

I managed to study with some of the great lights of the downtown theater world, including the brilliant actor and director Joe Chaiken, whose work centered on the inability of language to truly communicate the range of human experience, and Richard Schechner, well known for his work on ritual in performance inspired by the visionary anthropologist Victor Turner. These artists had been at the forefront of the experimental movement in the 1970s. As directors, they worked with companies of actors with whom they had something of a guru relationship, their seminal productions stretched the boundaries of conventional theater and were often reviled but much talked about. By the early 1980s that movement was in its death throes. The mood of New York theater was changing. Materialism had supplanted nihilism and we ETW acolytes, still yearning for the camaraderie of a group, were mostly left to our own devices, trying to catch the wave as it were, and make our mark. A group of us formed a loose collective.

We needed our own leader, and very quickly one of our fellow students emerged as our director. An Austrian, Peter attired himself in suits and pants held up with rope. He had something of a drug habit, smoked Gitanes, and regularly carried his belongings in a cardboard suitcase. Actually, he carried everything he owned as he didn't have a place to live and was squatting in the back of an art gallery. He appeared to have emerged straight out of a Beckett play and he was German! He named our group Boom. I didn't know what that meant then and I don't know now, but it did sound punk and it stuck.

The fact that he spoke German carried a lot of weight with us because the favored writers of the alienated included Brecht, Wedekind, and Büchner. German choreographers Pina Bausch and Anna Teresa De Keersmacher had been innovating a form of postmodern dance theater that was influencing us at the time as well. This was where the pot-smoking and massage came in. It was exhausting and exhilarating. We didn't work on traditional acting skills like diction, projection, and script interpretation; no, we were more interested in how bodies moved in space and spent hour after hour running, walking, and rolling around and dreaming up ways to make an audience work as hard as possible to understand what was being conveyed.

The first play our group, Boom, staged was an adaptation of Franz Kafka's short story "The Hunger Artist." The story was staged like a carnival sideshow. The audience was to be led past various exhibits, of which I was one. There was no real narrative; the concept was one of visiting an art gallery. I was attired in some type of torn tutu, perched in front of a cage and armed with a whip that I periodically brandished at one of our fellow cast members who crawled around the enclosure in a diaper. I had no lines. I growled.

My parents flew in to see me in my first New York production. They were so stunned they were simply speechless. I believe my mother wept. To say it was poorly received would imply that a number of people actually attended the performances. We did attract a smattering of fellow students and of course my parents, but that was it. Between my mother's distress and the fact that I got dates, I took that as a ringing endorsement of our artistic aesthetic.

Our next play was to be a meditation on the loss of innocence and the death of glamour. Or was it the loss of glamour and the death of innocence? I can't remember which one. Our group had been invited to perform at a downtown punk hole-in-the-wall, the Pyramid Club. We were booked as a weekly alternative soap opera, a popular concept at that time, with new installments to be staged every week.

Our first week saw our exploration of Innocence. I recall a scene in which a talented sprite of an actress and I were on stage and she was to get her period for the first time. This effect was to be achieved by breaking a sandwich baggie with ketchup in her panties. We never rehearsed this, but it seemed like something that would work. After several failed tries at clapping her legs together hard enough to break the bag, I believe I just reached over and squashed it myself which was greeted with hilarity from the audience. After that scene, the condimented actress and I laughed so hard in the subbasement dressing room that we vowed that we would always remember this as our worst moment on stage. We were wrong. That was yet to come.

The next week's installment focused on Glamour. Our characters were transformed into silent film stars slowly pantomiming death. There was supposed to be a silent black-and-white super 8 film accompanying us. We had been photographed frolicking in an abandoned lot dressed in vintage gowns. Unfortunately, the projector broke down, as did the tiny portable cassette player with our sound track. Ever resourceful, our director got up on the side of the stage and beat out a rhythm on a mop and pail. We sank to the floor at a snail's pace. People yelled, "Die already!!" throughout the entire half an hour it took to descend to the stage. The management refused to pay us. I thought it was a brilliant misunderstood message. We weren't invited back.

I was not deterred, however. Every rejection of our art reinforced my belief in our visionary work. The more people who disliked our work, the better. In fact, we roundly believed that once we achieved universal disdain, this would mean we had made our mark.

Our chance at the big time turned out to be right around the corner. Peter had received funding for us to stage *Mörder, Hoffnung der*

Frauen, a play so degenerate that Kokoschka had been briefly run out of town following its premiere. We were to perform in Vienna itself, in a restored old palace, and real Germanic people would join us in the cast. I was to play the lead role, Frau. I was in heaven. We could only hope to be as reviled as Oskar Kokoschka himself.

Triumph was at hand. From the moment I stepped on stage, the crowd booed. The crowd actually came to see theater with vegetables in tow. They threw lettuce heads, they chucked tomatoes, and they talked back to us in German. Unfortunately, my language skills were so limited I never understood what they were saying. When I swung a real dead chicken over my head as I paced inside my cage, the audience seemed just as confused as I was. But the play was about something important. Love, loss, poultry . . . it was exciting. We engaged in heated late-night discussions of the production in broken English, I took up with a local guy, drank *Kaffe mit Schlag*, and went to work each day in a palace.

By the time we all arrived back in NYC, we were sure we had an important work to share. We were invited to do the show at the Guggenheim Museum. It was the dead of winter. We had small polite audiences, mostly docents of the museum. No one threw vegetables, and after the shows the audience cleared out quickly and in silence. No late-night philosophizing and I got no dates. I trudged home in the snow each night alone. The one review we received was from the infamously cruel John Simon who wrote simply: *Why?*

That was the last show we all did together. We all drifted apart after the tepid reception to the play. I was crushed. There just was no future in it for me. Not enough people had rejected us to make our work really important. Rejection meant controversy, controversy meant press, press led to lucrative grants to continue our work. So I moved on. I started acting in television. My first two roles in nighttime TV were playing prostitutes on *Miami Vice* and *The Equalizer*. Though not literally in a cage, metaphorically, my characters were, so I felt quite at home, but my career in the avant-garde world was finished.

It should be noted that many ETWers have gone on to produce interesting work in many mediums. Nicky Silver's plays are regularly performed Off-Broadway. Our classmate Liz Tuccillo co-wrote a little book called *He's Just Not That Into You*. One fellow student is now the director of ETW; one instructor is a vice-president of Disney Theme Parks; she lives on my block in Los Angeles and our fairly well-groomed children are best friends. The two performers in that first work? One is a distinguished choreographer, the other a nightclub raconteur in Berlin. Her disaffected songs are very popular throughout that country. That director from Austria? We're still friends, and often meet up when he's in from Austria, where he directs very well received TV movies and raises his two beautiful children. The New York avant-garde scene had rejected us; perhaps, in the end, we were just a little *after* our time.

Actress and writer **Annabelle Gurwitch** is currently a commentator on *Day to Day* on NPR where she prognosticates on everything from science and politics to pop culture, and she has just been awarded her own humor column at TheNation.com. Best known to TV audiences for her many years co-hosting *Dinner and a Movie* on TBS, her essays have appeared in *The Los Angeles Times, Penthouse, Premiere,* and *Glamour,* among others. Annabelle's first book, *Fired! Tales of the Canned, Canceled, Downsized & Dismissed,* was deemed a "merry compendium of failure" by *The Washington Post,* and was #1 on the *New York Post* Hot List. *O, The Oprah Magazine,* called her documentary film on the same subject, "entertaining and slyly subversive," and *Newsday* exclaimed, "it's smart, funny and poignant." The film is currently in rotation on Showtime and the Sundance Channel.

Easy Money

Michael Schulman

The summer after my college graduation, I was unemployed and unqualified for basically everything. But what I lacked in experience I made up for in enthusiasm and low standards. I came across an ad on Craigslist that seemed promising: Someone was needed to distribute flyers for a "gay lifestyle website" at bars across the city. The information was vague, but I imagined the website was for some kind of dating service or soccer league or, even better, some sort of advocacy group. (To quote Joan Didion, "Was anyone ever so young?") The ad listed a phone number and offered modest compensation, and I figured, well, as long as I'm going to gay bars anyway, I might as well bring along flyers and make some money. The drinks would pay for themselves.

I contacted the man—let's call him Ted, because I've forgotten his name completely—who suggested that I meet him at his apartment in the East Village at 9 P.M. the following night. In retrospect, this was the first of many unheeded warning signs. I printed out a copy of my résumé, which noted that I was an English major and the valedictorian of my high school class and that I'd worked as a camp counselor and had intermediate Italian-language skills. "Intermediate" was probably a stretch, but I decided I would take my chances.

At the appointed hour I arrived at Ted's building, rode up a creaky elevator, and rang the bell. Ted was a genial, middle-aged man dressed in jeans and a T-shirt, and when he cracked open the door it was just wide enough for him to squeeze through and meet me in the hallway, which was small and purple and dimly lit. He shook my hand and asked me if I'd like to go up to the roof. I was wary, but said sure. On job interviews, first impressions are essential.

The roof was broad and dark, with a small oasis of patio furniture situated within an expanse of concrete. Ted sat me down and started off with some basic questions. How old was I? (22.) What were my interests? (Theater, travel.) What time commitment could I offer him? (My schedule was wide open.)

As I looked around it suddenly occurred to me that, for all I knew, Ted could be a serial rapist. What better way to lure young unsuspecting men to your apartment than under the guise of an "interview"? And where better to lead them than onto this secluded, unlit rooftop, where no one can hear you scream? I realized I should have given the address to a friend beforehand, so that if I happened to disappear they'd know where to send the search party. But it was too late for that; I'd have to keep my guard up and take note of the nearest exits. They say it's crucial during job interviews to maintain eye contact, but I don't think I looked him in the eyes once. I was too busy pondering my escape. The conversation turned extremely awkward.

I asked, timidly, "So, what exactly is your website for?"

"Well," he said, "I just recently started my own online business, which I'm still getting off the ground. It's basically a website for single men, but what I'm really hoping to do is expand the focus into culture and the arts. But that's a little bit down the road."

Interesting. Wait, what? I still had no idea what the website was for. I respected the fact that he was, ostensibly, an independent business owner, and my sense of being in immediate peril began to dissipate. But I was still uneasy. "Can I see one of the flyers?" I asked.

His eyes shifted. "I . . . have a couple in my apartment. Maybe I can get one for you on your way out."

We chatted for a few more minutes. He asked me to name some of my favorite gay bars in the city, and I consciously tried to pad my answer out to give a sense of geographical diversity. Why was I still trying to impress him? I suppose there was a part of me that didn't want to bomb the interview. I mean, I was a Yale English major—surely, I could nail this. I mentioned the fact that I was a Yale English major.

He shook my hand, took down my number, and led me back to the elevator. At this point, I figured the chances were slim that I would be raped and killed. And now I was really curious. In the elevator I asked him once again, "So, what is the website? What is it FOR?"

His eyes drifted toward the floor and he said haltingly, "It's a . . . spanking website."

"Oh, cool," I said, trying to strike a tone of genuine interest. He was clearly ashamed of his chosen field, so I thought it would be nice to lend him a little validation. "I would love to see the flyer," I said.

We got off on his floor. "Wait here," he said. Once again, he slipped through the door to his apartment without opening it fully, as if to avoid the possibility that I would get a glimpse inside. Gee, I thought, maybe someone is getting spanked in there right now. He came out with a glossy half-page flyer in his hand. "You can keep this," he said.

On the flyer was a picture of a man lying on his stomach, his toned buttocks in full view. Another man was kneeling beside him, naked, his hand outspread and poised mid-thwack. Above the picture, in thick, red letters, was the title "WWW.SPANKMEHARD .COM," along with the subheading, "Hot online spanking videos!!!"

I thanked Ted and headed out into the night. Looking back, I shouldn't have underestimated the importance of direct, confident eye contact. I never heard from Ted after that. I didn't get the job.

Michael Schulman's work has appeared in *The Believer* and in *The New Yorker*, where he is on the editorial staff. His other jobs have included teaching nursery school, reading opera librettos to the blind, and writing an auction catalogue of Civil War memorabilia. He lives in Manhattan.

Welcome to the Centaur Rodeo and My Female Protagonist

Sam Means

Both of these pieces were rejected by *The New Yorker* in 2006. It's a dream of many comedy writers (myself included) to get a humor piece published in the Shouts and Murmurs column, to join the ranks of Robert Benchley, Woody Allen, and James Thurber. Unfortunately, that's not an easy task. I've submitted several pieces over the past couple of years, and "Centaur Rodeo" is the closest I've ever come, since it was actually accepted before eventually getting killed. The folks over there are really nice, though, which makes it easier to take. The worst is when someone rejects something by just never writing back.

Welcome to the Centaur Rodeo

These are all real operation names from the Iraq War, which the editors ultimately decided were just too confusing. I actually got a kill fee for this one.

Coalition troops conducting Operation Centaur Rodeo to interdict weapons smugglers near Baqubah seized three people and netted numerous weapons March 30.
—U.S. Armed Forces Information Services press release, March 31, 2004

You've probably never heard of me, but I am an essential part of the U.S. war effort in the Middle East. I've never put on a Kevlar vest or looked through night vision binoculars—heck, I've never even been to Iraq—but the government depends on me to provide a vital service.

I'm in charge of taxonomy.

When the military needs something named, I'm their man, and I'm damn good at my job.

I was just out of grad school when the first Gulf War broke out. The call came in early August, and I was ready. I'd gotten my master's in wartime branding, with a minor in combat lexicography. Over the summer, I'd interned at a paintball range.

At the time, I had no idea where it would take me, but before I knew it *Operation Desert Shield* had blown up and I was the toast of Arlington, Virginia. After that it's all a blur: the money, the women, the secret medals . . . those were heady days.

But after we won and the first President Bush left office, there was a decade or so of relative peace over there, and I was out of a job. I brooded. I experimented. I perfected my craft.

And then I got the call. It was March 2003, and we were finally going back.

As I told the President, bring it on.

I started out slow. *Operation Iraqi Freedom* was a no-brainer, but soon the "peacekeeping operations" started piling up, and I had to dig deeper and deeper.

There was the "Iron" series, which I'm very proud of: Operations *Iron Force, Iron Fist, Iron Fury, Iron Grip, Iron Justice,* and, of course, *Iron Fist II: The Re-Fistening.* I guess that last subtitle got left off the official paperwork.

Operation O.K. Corral and *Operation Saloon* were a little more out there. I wanted to compare the desert in Iraq to the old west in Tombstone, Arizona. But harder-core, like if Wyatt Earp was a professional wrestler. I felt that I really captured the tone of the First Cavalry Division's search for insurgents in southern Baghdad with *Operation Tombstone Pile Driver.*

Not everyone got what I was going for, but it wasn't about being commercial. I realized that I had to be true to myself and to my vision, and that's when I really found my muse.

My first truly conceptual piece was *Operation Wolfpack Crunch*, the name I gave to a little reconnaissance mission in Diwaniya. It ruffled some feathers, sure, but the name *Wolfpack Crunch* really captured what I was feeling at the time: peyote-fueled rage.

During that period, I explored the bounds of wartime taxonomy, and I think I took the genre to some interesting places. Operations *Phantom Linebacker, Cajun Mousetrap,* and *Moon River Dragon* all spoke to the disorientation of the common soldier, and *Operation Grizzled Forced Entry* was an exploration of my own repressed memories from childhood.

Not every mission was a home run, of course. *Operation Restoring Rights* doesn't seem to be going anywhere, but you can hardly blame me for that. I did get into a little trouble for *Operation Suicide Kings,* though. The brass thought it sent the wrong message. That just wasn't a very good movie, Christopher Walken or no Christopher Walken.

But other than that they gave me a lot of creative freedom, thanks to my earlier success . . . and a general lack of oversight.

I felt I had the opportunity to really do something. If *Desert Storm* was my *Dark Side of the Moon,* then it was time for me to unleash my *The Wall.* (Interesting side-note: If you read the list of my peace-keeping operations in chronological order, it syncs up perfectly with *The Wizard of Oz.*)

In 2004, I released my most personal and experimental work to date to both commercial and critical success. Within days, *Operation Centaur Rodeo* was all over the radio: Hannity, Limbaugh, O'Reilly, you name it. The operation helped to staunch the flow of illegal weapons in Baqubah, but more importantly, the name *Centaur Rodeo* was a hit. It even swept the 2005 Oppies.

Shortly thereafter, U.S. forces technically handed over sovereignty to the new Iraqi government, and since then our operations in the region haven't been on the same scale. There's been work here and there (I'm especially proud of the Kafkaesque *Operation Phantom Fury*), but they've been more concerned lately with "reconstruction" than with operations like *Striker Tornado* or *Ivy Blizzard*.

It's just as well, I suppose. I needed a break from the grind. With the next war more than four months away, I've got some time now to sit back with my feet in the sand, drinking Coronas and thinking about the best name for our next invasion. *Operation Nuclear Summer* is what I'm working with for the time being.

I'll figure it out, though. I always do.

My Female Protagonist

(I think the *New Yorker* may have been uncomfortable with the phrase "on the rag.")

I really believe that since "writer" is a term without gender, a good one should be able to write believable male and female characters.
—Nora Roberts

Excerpts from my detective novel, *A Murder Most Frilly.*

Chapter 1

I was sitting in my bedroom one day, painting my toenails, when someone burst into the house.

"You're my only hope," he gasped, as he fell toward me.

It was Jason, my homosexual confidante. But before he could reach me, he was dead, with two bullet holes in his back.

"Eek!" I screamed. "Blood!"

Chapter 3

"You might be asking why I called you all here together," I told the assembled group. "It's because one of the people in this room is the murderer.

"Also, because I wanted to ask you what you think of this pretty dress I just bought. It's Donna Karan."

Chapter 4

Something was wrong. I knew from my woman's intuition that one of these people wasn't telling the truth. It just didn't add up, much like my checkbook.

At an impasse like this, there was only one thing to do: spa day!

Chapter 7

The killer had slipped through my fingers again. Maybe I just wasn't cut out for detective work. The only thing I seem to be any good at is spending my husband's hard-earned money.

Chapter 12

One thing was becoming painfully clear: Whoever killed Jason was also in possession of the computer disk. Whatever was on that disk must have been pretty important. Important enough to kill for.

The police hadn't found any fingerprints in Jason's office, but maybe it was time for a second look. After watching a couple of episodes of *Sex and the City* on DVD and eating a big piece of chocolate cake, I was ready to tackle the case anew.

Chapter 13

I came to on the floor of the office with a splitting headache and a growing sense that I was in way too deep. When I looked down, things just got worse: I had broken a nail.

Even though I had no intention of letting him have sex with me, I called and woke up my college friend Steven for a ride home, because I knew that he would do anything I asked him to.

Chapter 18

As I chased the killer through the streets of the French Quarter, my nipples were erect with excitement. Bounce, bounce, bounce went my womanly breasts while I ran down the narrow streets in my high-heeled shoes.

At the end of the alley he turned around to face me, and I saw that the man who knocked me unconscious in Jason's office, the man who stole the computer disk, and the man who nearly toppled the entire Canadian government, was the one man I had thought was already dead.

I was staring Jason right in the face, and he desperately needed his pores scrubbed.

Chapter 20

Luckily, I had made a copy of the disk before he got away. I went upstairs and changed while my assistant Brendan decoded the files.

"Do I look fat in this?" I asked him when I came back down.

"No," he answered.

"Are you saying that I look fat normally, just not in this particular outfit?"

After a brief argument we were off to deliver the evidence to the FBI.

Chapter 25

Watching the Lieutenant Governor led away in handcuffs, I felt a deep sense of relief, but I knew that it wasn't over. I had to find Jason. Only then could I finally get what I wanted more than anything else in the world: a baby.

Chapter 27

I had all but given up hope, trapped in the hull of that abandoned ship. When I heard rats scurrying across the floor I became hysterical, but thankfully Brendan was there to slap some sense into me.

Chapter 28

We had worked together so long, I never noticed what it seemed everyone else already knew. Brendan and I were falling in love.

At first I resisted Brendan's strong, manly hands, even though I actually longed for his embrace. My mouth said "No," but my eyes said "Yes! Yes! Yes!"

Chapter 31

It looks like Jason outsmarted me again, but at least the city is safe again, for now. I might have been able to stop him once and for all, but unfortunately I'm just a woman.

And it doesn't help that I was probably on the rag.

Sam Means is an Emmy-winning staff writer for *The Daily Show with Jon Stewart,* a cartoonist for *The New Yorker,* and a former contributing writer for *The Onion.* He is the author, as C.H. Dalton, of the book *A Practical Guide to Racism.*

What a Catch

Katina Corrao

Once upon a time I met an amazing guy. He was *so* amazing that after three days he told me that he loved me. He *loved* me! How lucky I was to meet such a spectacular guy! But he did want to make one thing clear. He never wanted to be my "boyfriend." I was never to use that word. He just didn't like it. But he was so awesome! What a catch! I mean, sometimes he would promise he would call and then sort of forget, and, well, there was this one time when he kinda sorta called me by his ex-girlfriend's name. There was more hair on his back than from the head of every Breck Girl who ever walked the earth . . . and he wanted yours truly to shave it. (I know. I know.) So, he makes a date with me for a Saturday night. The only thing was that he asked me not to bother him that whole week before our date because he said he was going to be super-busy at work. And I understood because I totally know how busy baristas can get. So I agreed.

He turned his cell phone off (randomly), but I called anyway just to listen to his dreamy voice mail message on his cell. By Friday, I was sure that he was going to call me or email me or something just to secure our plans but he didn't. Was he okay? I wondered if he was okay. I hoped he was okay. So I tried his cell phone and it rang this time but he didn't pick up. I figured something was wrong. Maybe he fell. So, I emailed him. He didn't respond. So, I emailed him again because I just wanted to make sure that he got it because sometimes email is weird. He didn't respond. Oh God, did he die? I called his cell phone twenty-seven more times and he didn't answer. So then I sent him a text message. He didn't respond. I tried to relax. I didn't want to jump to conclusions but a thought did sort of cross my mind. Maybe, even though it was a crazy thought, that he was avoiding me? No, he would never do that to me. I tried his work phone and he didn't answer. Then I remembered that he had Caller ID at his work. So I dialed * something or other before I dialed his number so I would make my number private over the Caller ID and then I would be able to see whether or not he was avoiding me. This time, when my number came across as private, he picked up! He was alive! He was avoiding me, but he was alive! I said, "Hi sunshine, it's me! Are you okay?" He said, "Yeah, why?" I said, "Well, I couldn't reach you and—" then he cut me off and said, "Listen I am super-busy, can I call you right back?" He never called back. Saturday night, the night of our big date, came and went. I got my nails done anyway just in case he surprised me. He didn't. No calls. No emails. Not one text. Nothing. A few days later he sent me an email.

Katina,

Listen up, here's the deal. i've been working night and day the last few days. Which means, that i've been working my butt off and operating on very little sleep. i can't just drop what i'm doing to email or make personal phone calls right now.

I haven't even talked to my family. i really can't take this anymore. i'm honestly at my wits end. i need to get outta hear, stat. i apologize for being distant. i just don't feel like talking to anyone. i hope you can understand. can we pretend for a second that i'm not a horrible bastard? And now my stupid ex-girlfriend wants to date me again. And i just don't want to. So yes, it is me. I'm not denying it. believe it or not, i'm not in the "hurting feelings" business So I'm sorry if you think I'm being insensitive, but I have priorities, Testy McFarland. I'm very sorry but in typical Katina fashion, you have freaked out, yet again. I'm sorry, but this is just too much. I really hope you're ok. But I'm not the person for you to turn to. I'm sorry, but I don't think a romantic relationship or friendship itself will ever work. Good luck with everything.

Take care.

I never responded. But, I am not going to lie and tell you that being rejected by him like that, over an email, didn't burst my heart into a billion little bits. Didn't he have fun with me? I mean, I took an interest in his career . . . I *love* coffee. A couple of years later my friend bumped into him at a deli. He told her that he was looking for another job. Apparently he wanted out of the caffeine business altogether. Then, she said that he *asked about me!* Can you believe it? She said that he said, "How's Katina?" *What?* What does he mean "How am I"? What, so now he just wants to know how I am all the time? What is he, obsessed with me or something? It's just so random, right? Yeah, like I'm so sure it would even work out between the two of us. I mean, just because I still know his phone number by heart doesn't mean anything. It was an easy number to memorize. But, I shouldn't call him, right? Ha-ha . . . I'm just kidding. But can you believe it? He asked about me? He *asked* about me!

See? I told you he was amazing!

Katina Corrao is a graduate of Cabrini College and The American Conservatory Theatre's Summer Training Congress in San Francisco, California. After graduation, she moved to New York City and began performing with the Upright Citizens Brigade Theatre. Katina is the writer and performer of her one-person show, *Italian Cookies: A Recipe of Love and Anxiety,* and the two-person sketch show, *The Matt and Katina Show!,* and co-creator of *Mending your Life with Rita and Wilma.* She is also the co-host/producer of *Cabaret Star!,* in which she plays the lovable Sparkle Montgomery, and a member of the musical improv group *The Pearl Brunswick.* Katina has served as the warm-up comic for several of New York City's top shows and has been seen on HBO, Current TV, *One Life to Live, The Late Show with David Letterman, Cash Cab, Late Night with Conan O'Brien,* and *Saturday Night Live.* She has been a commentator on VH1's *Best Night Ever* and is a featured style comic in the weekly magazine *Life & Style.*

Fly

Kate Flannery

I wrote "Fly" after I finally broke up with my ex-boyfriend who put me in
financial hell.

I am a fly. So I fly. I have so much freedom I don't know what to do
with it. I am a fly and I am attracted to shit. I've hung around shit. I've
fallen in love with shit. I was stuck with shit until it rained so hard on
it that the shit got washed away and I was on my own again with my
freedom. Too much freedom. I am a fly. I fly everywhere, but I get
stuck in rooms. For days I fly everywhere in the room trying to act
free but desperately trying to find a way out. I get slow and silly until
the universe sends me a breeze and I'm out the door with my freedom. Too much freedom. I'm a fly. I've been shooo-ed and swatted
and I've survived. I've been attracted to bright, bright light. I've
buzzed around the light and when I got close I burned myself. Thank
God the light burns out and I'm free again. I am a fly. I get stuck between the window and the screen. I get stuck in the tight space. I don't
give up. I feel the light, I get tired but I get used to being stuck. I feel
safe from harm's way. But the seasons change and the screens get
taken down and I am free again. Too free. I am a fly. So I fly . . .

Kate Flannery plays Meredith on NBC's *The Office*. Her comedy lounge act,
The Lampshades, has been running in Hollywood at the Improv Olympic

West stage for over four years and was seen at the U.S. Comedy Arts Festival in Aspen. Kate's other TV work includes *The Bernie Mac Show, Boomtown, Curb Your Enthusiasm, Jimmy Kimmel Live!,* Comedy Central's *Crossballs,* and she was the voice of Lucy in a Robert Smigel cartoon on *SNL.* Kate graduated from the University of the Arts in Philadelphia where her family owns a bar.

Hackett Q&A

Joel Stein

I used to do Q&As for *Time* magazine, where my goal was to be a dick. Thing is, being a dick took a fair amount of work: I read everything available on the person, picked out obscure facts, and related them to the one thing I cared about—me. The other thing is, about 10% of the time the person I was Q-ing didn't find my being a dick either fun or amusing. And I hate confrontation. So 10% of the time my stomach hurt and I vowed to never do another one. But then my boss would ask for one, and my stomach would feel better by then so I'd do it anyway. It's the same psychological process that allows women to get pregnant again after experiencing the pain of childbirth. Only instead of a child who I would love for the rest of my life, I got a Q&A with Buddy Hackett.

My editor at *Time* didn't want to run this because it ends abruptly. That's mostly because Hackett hangs up on me. This was one of several arguments I had with my editor in which I took the position that the phrase "hangs up" is the best possible ending for a Q&A. I think I may have used Aristotle to make my point. She never went for it. She felt that "hangs up," far from providing closure, made all parties concerned look bad. She didn't realize that was my entire point.

Buddy Hackett

Buddy Hackett plays a chauffeur on Fox's *Action*.[1]

1. This took place in August of 1999, right before the critically acclaimed, publicly ignored Jay Mohr sitcom *Action* came out on Fox.

Q: Hello, this is Joel.

A: This is Buddy Hackett.

Q: Wow.[2] Thanks for calling. I was wondering if we could still do the interview tomorrow like it was planned, if you can. I haven't prepared any questions yet.

A: Okay. But let's talk now for an hour[3] and maybe that will help for tomorrow.

Q: Okay.[4] When's the last time you had a Tuscan Yogurt Pop?[5]

A: The last time I did a commercial.

Q: But you weren't eating them at home, were you?

A: Fuck I wasn't. It was delicious. The man who owned Tuscan had some brothers or cousins who were partners and they went with Dick Van Patten, and the sales kind of disappeared.

Q: Who wants to buy a yogurt pop from Dick Van Patten?[6]

A: You know you're being kind of, what do you call it, I don't know, those wise-guy papers? Tabloids. You're being a little tabloid with me here and I don't really like that very much. So don't do that.

Q: Okay.[7]

---

2. Hackett's publicist had scheduled a call for the following afternoon, so this was indeed surprising. Luckily, none of my friends can do an impression of a really old, heavy-set man with a childlike voice. Otherwise, I would have thought it was a prank. Like I did with NBC CEO Jeff Zucker.

3. An hour? These Q&As were one-third of a page. They usually took about twenty minutes. This was where I completely messed up. I didn't understand that Hackett, who no longer did many interviews, just wanted to talk about himself, and it was my job to let him.

4. I seem to understand what's going on and will just listen and take notes for tomorrow. Instead, for reasons I'm not clear on (Did I think he wouldn't call the next day? Did I want to record as much Hackett material as I could for some kind of Hackett Q&A book?), I quickly attached my tape recorder and started asking whatever dick questions I could think of.

5. Like anyone who was twenty-eight at the time, the yogurt pop commercials were the only thing I knew about Buddy Hackett.

6. That's the dick part. I have nothing against Dick Van Patten. In fact, I loved *Eight Is Enough*. Especially the actress who played Elisabeth.

7. This implies that I understand that an old Jew just wants to talk about his life for a while. You think, as a person who grew up with old Jews, I would get that. I did not.

A: Also, don't do wise-guy things to me.

Q: What do you mean?[8]

A: Like "Who wants to buy a pop from Dick Van Patten?" You're trying to get me to commit to one of your ideas. I'm not going to do that.

Q: Well, I'll try to come up with smart, non-wise-guy questions tomorrow.[9]

A: God, there's so many other things that are important. Are you just looking for a humorous story?[10]

Q: What's more important?

A: How to get along in life. How to find a sense of values that are important and stay with them.[11]

Q: This isn't right. Buddy Hackett shouldn't be getting all serious on me.[12]

A. I'm not getting serious on you. I'm just a very smart person.

Q: Well, I'll call . . .[13]

A: I've met a couple of women who had higher IQs than I do, and I was really bemused by it. Jill St. John has 162. And there was a girl, a dancer in a show I was in on Broadway, her name was Morocco. And she had over 180.

Q: Did you not expect women to have high IQs?[14]

---

8. I wasn't being disingenuous. I couldn't believe he was calling me out when I was only at about 4 percent dick level. I was saying that only he could represent Tuscan Yogurt Pops effectively. I was knocking Dick Van Patten, not him. And I was prophetic about Van Patten. The guy would go on to eat dog food on infomercials for Natural Balance, a high-end dog food.

9. For a second, I get it. Just let him talk, and make sure he calls again tomorrow.

10. Well, you're a comedian. In a situation comedy. So, no. I'm looking for ethical philosophy from Buddy Hackett.

11. He, too, is thinking ethical philosophy.

12. Here is where I realize that I'm not just a dick for the purpose of the Q&A. I'm just actually a dick.

13. And I want to save my dickishness for the real interview.

14. This time, I was actually just shocked. How can I let that go? I wouldn't have let my grandfather get away with that.

A: I didn't say that, did I?

Q: You said you were surprised there were women who had higher IQs than you.[15]

A: No. Meaning two people who had higher IQs than I did.

Q: How high is your IQ?

A: 150.

Q: When did you have that tested?

A: When I was a child.

Q: You haven't had it retested?[16]

A: In the army, whatever the ATC was, you needed 110 to be an officer and I had 137.

Q: So you dropped from 150 to 137?

A: No. It's a different kind of test.

Q: But the same scoring system.

A: I doubt it very much. The army doesn't do the same as anybody else. They dig a well by going up.

Q: What?

A: You're in bad shape, kid. They dig a well by going up.[17] Where'd you go to school?

Q: To college?[18]

A: No. I don't know anything about college.[19]

Q: I went to a public school in New Jersey called J.P. Stevens in Edison.

A: Edison is a very pretty town. Very clean. Very lawned. It's out of a picture book.

---

15. Suddenly, I'm Tim Russert. Answer the question, Mr. Hackett!

16. I do think IQ tests are kind of stupid, and especially skewed for children.

17. I still don't really get that.

18. This is a particularly obnoxious thing people who went to good colleges do. You asked about my intelligence and then my schooling. Do you perhaps mean college? Or do you want to know about my elementary schooling?

19. Honestly, I think he wasn't asking where I went to college.

Q: The malls are very nice.

A: The malls weren't built when I was there. I was there fifty years ago.

Q: What did people do before malls?

A: People sat in the backyard and talked to each other. I lived in Leonia, New Jersey, and next door to me was a guy named Anderson. He had a son. He was the cutest kid. And he'd walk in and suddenly show up in the kitchen and his opening line would be, "Guess what we're having for dinner tonight?" And we'd say, "What are you having?" And he'd say, "T'ompany."[20]

Q: You have this reputation for being a dirty comic and you're telling me cute little stories about kids. What happened?[21]

[Buddy Hackett hangs up.]

Joel Stein is desperate for attention. He grew up in Edison, New Jersey, went to Stanford, and then worked for Martha Stewart for a year. After two years of fact checking at various publications, he got hired as a sports editor at *Time Out New York*. Two years later he lucked into a job as a staff writer for *Time* magazine where he gained notice for his arch celebrity Q&As and for his anecdotal humor columns. After teaching a class in humor writing at Princeton, he moved to Los Angeles at the beginning of 2005 to write a column for the *Los Angeles Times* and work as a sitcom writer. Being desperate for attention, he can sometimes be seen as a talking head on television programs such as VH1's *I Love the 80s*, HBO's *Phoning It In*, Comedy Central's *Reel Comedy*, and E! Entertainment's *101 Hottest Hot Hotties' Hotness*. He also co-produced three TV pilots, an animated series for VH1, and two for ABC. The animated show, titled *Hey Joel*, aired only in Canada, while the other two were never picked up.

20. This story took a good five minutes. I must have cut it down severely for space.
21. I thought I was being un-dickish right here. I was wrong.

Brother Elk

Neal Pollack

I wrote this short story a couple of years ago while I was living in Austin, Texas, and then I sent it around to a bunch of magazines, all of which rejected it. These included glossy magazines that had written me asking for a short story. You know you're in trouble when the editor writes you looking for something "fresh and surprising," since most glossy magazines never print anything that's remotely close to either. But I also got rejected by literary magazines like *Tin House*. In retrospect, *Tin House* probably wasn't the best place for a short story that includes a rape scene on the hood of a car in the parking lot of an Elks Lodge. But what did I know? I wanted to get the thing published. At least *Tin House* politely told me no. Most publications asked for a submission, took that submission, and never contacted me again.

Reading it now, the story seems maybe a little heavy-handed in places, but I still think it's good, part of my ongoing literary revenge against contemporary notions of "coolness." Of late, my pieces have been getting published in books of crime fiction. The audience for such work is so small that I can basically write whatever I want without fear of offending anyone. I hope Brother Elk someday follows in that tradition. Now then, ladies and gentlemen, I present: Brother Elk.

Early one Friday evening in November, when the weather was nice enough to attend an informal ceremony outside in a Misfits T-shirt and a pair of weathered pea-green cargo shorts, Holly LaTour, a thirty-two-year-old record-company publicist with no interest in permanent romantic attachment, became an official member of Elks

Lodge 1707 in Austin, Texas. Holly was the 137th new member inducted into the Lodge that year. By contrast, there had only been 324 previous members since the Lodge's inception in the mid-1920s. The Elks had first caught Holly's attention six months previous, when she'd attended a *Vice* magazine party at the Lodge building during South by Southwest. First, she noticed the view.

You could see the entire city from up that mount, as well as twenty miles of temperate hill country only occasionally punctuated by the country estates of retired hippies with connections in the real-estate industry. What a place for a party. But added value arrived in the moderately charming Lodge structure itself, built in the mid-1960s by a local architect who'd seen a *CBS News* profile of Frank Lloyd Wright. It had at least three levels, vaguely cantilevered. Occasionally, a glass antechamber protruded from a corner to lighten the mood.

The interior suffered from simultaneous over- and underuse. Holly didn't think that the Elks sufficiently appreciated the retroactive aesthetic appeal of concrete walls and wood paneling. She also felt it was a waste to have three spacious ballrooms that rarely hosted an event more glamorous than a bachelor-party poker game. The décor of the main hall consisted largely of hunting trophies and license plates, no one had added songs to the jukebox since 1976, and the hairspray selection in the ladies room had long passed its point of maximum kitsch value. If you joined, the beer was cheap and you could use the pool whenever you wanted.

One night, Holly met her friend Lisa for drinks in the lobby of a newly renovated motel.

"I went to a party the other night at the Elks Lodge," Lisa said.

"Oh yeah," Holly said. "I've been there."

"The people there are kind of weird and old—but cool. Totally regular people like someone you'd meet at the gas station. The building, on the other hand, is unbelievable."

"I know," Holly said. "I've been wanting to go back."

"You totally can!" Lisa said. "All you have to do is be the guest of a member. And guess what?"

"What?"

"I'm a member!" Lisa said. "They just ask you three or four questions, you give them thirty dollars, and you're in!"

"You joined the Elks Lodge?" Holly said. "Come on. That's like something my grandpa would have done."

The joiner gene ran more dominant in Holly's blood than she would have guessed. From the moment she walked through the door of the Elks Club on Lisa's arm, she felt like she belonged, though that may have been because she'd been hanging out with three-quarters of the people in the room her entire adult life. The New Elks had been born. Holly needed to get in on the action before everyone else found out and ruined the good time of those who'd been there first.

So, on that November night, she faced the Elks Council, who happened to be a retired beer-distribution company executive named Roger; Judith, plain, crude, and brash, who owed her high position to the national Elks leadership that her blessed late father had provided in the 1950s; and Melvin Huber, the Lodge's guiding spirit, a master of barbecue, and a secret part-time dealer of organic homegrown marijuana. Holly sat around a table with them and drank Miller Genuine Draft from a can. The fact that the beer had only cost a dollar only enhanced her already high enthusiasm.

"I tell you what," Melvin said. "I've got to be the luckiest sonofabitch in the world. Look around you. I was captain of a leaky catfish boat. And man, when you get out there in the middle of a lake and your boat starts to leak, you're always saying, 'Oh, man, now how am I gonna plug this up?' You know what I mean?"

"Sure," Holly said.

"Then all y'all started coming by, and everyone was complaining. You know, here come these yuppies and their grand ideas to remake us in their image and such, but I was like, 'Look around. Are you out of your mind?' This might be our last chance to hang out with ladies that are good-looking."

Holly laughed, and, to her great surprise, found herself oddly charmed. She blushed more than she should have and shifted her legs unconsciously but strategically. Melvin scratched his chin with a modest amount of thoughtfulness.

"Shit," he said. "I don't really need to ask you any questions. Isn't that right, guys?"

"Well," said Judith, "I did kinda want to know if Ms. LaTour intends to . . ."

"It's settled then!" Melvin said.

He extended a hand to Holly, and she took it, making sure to almost but not quite match his grip.

"Welcome to the Elks."

Roger scratched his neck and, with the other hand, reached into the pocket of his fifteen-year-old blue jeans. Out came two dollars. He handed them to Holly.

"Congratulations," he said. "Now be a good girl and go get us two beers so we can celebrate in style."

Holly's induction party didn't go as late as she wanted, because the Elks had a strict 2 A.M. shutdown policy. Other than that, it didn't disappoint. Her friends The Lucky Bastards, some of whom were Elks themselves, had played a full set in their trademark style, a kind of glam-rock/hillbilly boogie hybrid. Larch, the lead singer and Holly's former platonic screwbuddy, wore his eight-inch silver glitter platform shoes just for her. The Old Elks, what few of them were in the house, mostly sat at the bar or worked the steam table, dishing out two-dollar plates of barbecue with store-bought coleslaw. The New Elks filled one ballroom entirely and spilled out into the second, reveling in the advantages of their new association, occasionally heading out to the poolside grove to touch tongues and swap cell-phone numbers.

By closing time, all the guests had either migrated to that night's chosen afterparty or home to rest up for the next morning's Bloody Mary brunch. Holly left last, taking the steps down into the foyer very carefully, one at a time, while hanging onto the guardrail. She'd gotten stinking drunk; she could usually hold ten beers without too much trouble, but on this night she'd lost count. She blundered through the parking lot toward her mint-green 1977 DeVille.

"My carry car car car," she said to herself. "I love that car. It's my baby."

The moon went behind a patchwork cloud, dotting the parking lot with little laser glints of gray-white light. One of those beams was the only reason Holly saw Roger in the woods, just a few feet away from her front bumper. There was another Elk with him, but Holly hadn't yet learned that one's name.

"I think you'd better let me drive," Roger said.

"Oh," Holly said. "Hey. No. I'm OK. It's only five blocks. And I drive around trashed all the time. Everyone does."

He took a step forward. His hand reached the door handle at the same time that hers did. The other Elk was right behind.

"Lloyd and me want to take you for a ride," he said. "As part of your welcome to our club."

"I don't think . . ." she said.

His hand closed with a grip that meant under-the-table business.

"You don't have a choice," he said. "Now we can either get in the car or you can lay down on the hood. But I imagine that you'd probably prefer some cushion."

Holly really had to pee. They drew a tight circle around her. Lloyd got his hand on her blouse, which she'd bought at a cute little shop in New York the last time she'd visited there. A great boom sounded behind them, echoing off the high canyon walls.

Melvin stood in the entrance to the Elks Lodge, holding a shotgun above his head. He'd flooded the parking lot with security lights, which should have been on anyway; smoke wafted around him, like he was a magician who could manifest himself with a round of buckshot. He brought the gun to eye level, extended, and began walking forward.

"Jeeeee-zus Christ, Roger!" he said. "Man, you have got yourself some real bad manners! Here we have a fine young lady, the best in years, who has agreed, against what now looks like her better judgment, to bind herself to us by contract. But you can't seem to sheathe it. You think you're some kind of a prize or something?"

"No, Melvin," Roger said.

Melvin had reached them.

"Damn right," he said. "No wonder your wife doesn't let you wet the pony anymore. Who the hell wants anything to do with a pervert who hangs out in parking lots?"

He turned to Holly.

"Ma'am," he said. "I distinctly apologize for the terrible behavior exhibited by these gentlemen this evening."

"That's OK," Holly said.

"Beer ain't no excuse," Melvin said. "We've all raised a little hell because of beer. Shit. I once took a piss on the mayor's dog, and I didn't apologize, either. But there's raising hell and then there's doin' things that're gonna get you sent to hell. You're lucky she's only my Elk sister, and not my real sister, Roger, or else raccoons would be licking your brains off the asphalt by now!"

He put the barrel in Roger's face.

"Isn't that right, Roger-boy?" he said.

Roger nodded palely as Melvin swung the barrel around.

"And Lloyd?"

"Sure, Melvin," he said.

Melvin gave the gun a little wag.

"Now get your sorry little asses back to your sorry little suburban pickup trucks, and take next month's dues with you. For now, you're suspended. I'll decide later whether or not I want to boot you permanently."

They stood there blankly. Melvin raised the gun, cocked it at the trees just over their heads, and fired again. A bird's nest fell.

"Move!" he said.

They ran like the hunted. Melvin put the gun down and turned his attention back to Holly, who was very close to passing out. She leaned against him for support.

"Dang, girl," he said. "Maybe we need to set a lower limit for you."

"I'll be fine," she said.

She looked up at him sweetly.

"Thank you," she said.

"It wasn't nothing," Melvin said. "You're my Sister Elk and I'm sworn to protect you."

"Aw," she said.

"Say," said Melvin. "We're having a charity blackjack game next week. We kind of need an extra dealer. You willing to help out?"

"I don't know what's going on next week yet," Holly said.

"Come on, Sister," Melvin said. "Do it for the Elks."

Melvin walked over to where the nest had fallen. As he bent down, his eyes brightened. He held up something cream-colored and oval, flecked with brown specks.

"Well, I'll be danged," he said. "Lark eggs! Man, you can scramble these up and have yourself a *fine* little omelet, I tell you what."

Holly didn't hear him. She'd fallen asleep in her front seat after nearly vomiting into a cluster of pine needles. Melvin covered her with his jacket and stood watch until she woke up nearly an hour later.

For the next six months, Holly enjoyed the full benefits of her Elks membership. The Lodge proved the perfect setting for pre-parties, and for post-parties. When the weather turned sunbathe-worthy, around the first of March, she and her friends slathered up with UV protector and lay on the grass around the pool. The Lodge really needed to invest in some new lounge chairs, she thought. One of Holly's good friends owned a boutique that sold bikinis in the retro style but with even more subtle coverage. They were at the forefront of leisure fashion, spending a tenth of what a weekend in Palm Springs would have cost. Why live anywhere else?

Every afternoon, as she and her friends increased their risk of skin cancer by 40%, Holly boasted about her fine relationship with Melvin Huber, who she now called her "Brother Elk."

"I just want to treat my Brother Elk with the respect he deserves," she said.

"He's a fine man," Lisa said. "So well-connected."

"Without a doubt he's got the best weed in town," said the woman who owned the bathing-suit boutique. "He should run for mayor."

"I don't even think about that stuff," said Holly. "To me, he's just my Brother Elk."

Holly did what Melvin asked of her. If anything, his requests had increased her social desirability. She and her friends made monthly Blackjack Night into something exclusive, and therefore glamorous, and therefore fun. No dealer drew more players to a table. The men thought they were being boldly impressive by giving to charity, but really, they were just giving to charity; very little impressed Holly. She'd been making men throw good money after bad for years.

After one Blackjack Night, where Holly had, absurdly, outdrawn the other tables by nearly $3,000, Melvin approached her with a fresh proposal.

"I tell you what, Sister Elk," he said. "You got a fine thing going on there."

"Anything for the Elks," she said.

"Just the thought of getting a little titty turns men into morons."

"Don't I know it," said Holly.

"Now, I've seen too much to be really affected. Used to be when you went to a show in this town, all the chicks took off their shirts, and kept them off all night. I didn't mind that. Hell, I was just some dumb country boy, and it was like I'd walked into a store full of the most delicious candy in the world. I'm lucky I got anything done. Actually, I never did get anything done. But I guess my point here is that it's just titty, and I'm not gonna go slapping $1,000 on the table when I can get it anytime I want for free at home."

"Oh, Brother Elk," Holly said.

Melvin always made her laugh.

"You ever think of tending bar here a couple nights a week?" he said. "Judith's been wanting to cut back since her ankle surgery."

"Not really," she said. "I'm pretty busy at work as it is."

"Now I can certainly understand that," Melvin said. "I spend a lot of my day working, too. But I never forget that I've taken a pledge to uphold the standards of the Elks. To me, the Lodge comes first."

He winked.

"It's almost like I owe my life to the Elks or something," he said.

At that moment, Holly realized that Melvin's motives might house ulterior elements, though she couldn't pinpoint what they were or how he'd arrived at them. Regardless, she began working eight to midnight on Wednesday and nine to close on Fridays. She didn't mind so much. It was much better than her past bartending experiences, sort of like hanging out with her friends for tips. If anything, the parties got more intense. Beer distributors started stopping by the Lodge three times a week. In fact, Holly was able to pinpoint, as she often did, the exact moment that the scene peaked. It happened about fifteen minutes after she served a gin and tonic to a reporter from the alt-weekly who'd stopped by to research a piece on the Elks "phenomenon."

Two weeks later, the weekly's cover story bore this lead: "It's a little past 11 P.M. on a Friday night, but the Elks Lodge is hopping. And not just with the usual collection of aging war veterans, either. No, for the last year, the Elks have been quietly increasing their membership by hooking up with some of this town's most well-connected partiers."

The dagger was inserted. Then the reporter twisted it, and yet another good time lost its edge forever.

"This is not your father's Elks Club," he wrote.

On a Friday evening at an outdoor coffeehouse where The Lucky Bastards were putting on a free show, Holly read the piece and thought: Why do journalists have to ruin everything?

That night at work, Melvin felt differently. He whooped when Holly showed him the paper. He held it up like a hunting trophy.

"Goddamn!" he said. "Will you look at this? I never thought I'd see my name in the newspaper! Well, I did see my name in it once, but that's what you get when you drop acid, paint yourself silver, and run naked through the foyer of the State Capitol. I was young. Anyway, this is the best dang publicity the Elks could ever get!"

"I do publicity for a living," Holly said, "and I'll have to disagree with you there."

A few hours later, Holly faced an empty cash drawer and a half-dozen couples slow dancing to a scratchy recording of "I Fall To Pieces." Judith sat drinking a bourbon and water. She didn't have any trouble hanging out on the other side of the bar. Melvin approached. He'd drunk a few himself.

"Must be something else going on tonight," he said.

"Not really," Holly said.

"Oh well," he said. He took a long pull from the can. "More beer for me, then!"

Holly stared ahead glumly.

"Hey, Sister Elk?" he said.

"Yes, Brother Elk?" she said.

"I really need some help cleaning out my shed tomorrow morning."

"Tomorrow's bad for me," she said.

"What about Sunday?"

"I like to keep my weekends pretty open."

Judith coughed.

"You know, Melvin," she said. "It's almost like people don't appreciate it when you save them from getting gang-raped anymore."

"Now Judith," Melvin said. "You know I don't like to talk about that."

Melvin looked at Holly, cocked his head, and threw her an almost imperceptible smile that would never stand up in court as threatening.

"I'll come by at ten," Holly said.

The Elks waned. But Holly kept working at the Lodge anyway. When friends would tease her, asking why she'd hung on, she'd say something moderately ironic, like, "It's my Elkly duty." But the real answer would have been "because the Lodge President keeps me continually on guard with his subtle insinuations of emotional blackmail." Even if she'd told them that, they would just have said, "There goes Holly with her men again."

Sure, but this one was different. For one thing, Melvin had never even came close to making a sexual advance on her. He'd sometimes entertain the Lodge with a tale of sexual mirth; for example, he spent one night telling everyone about how he banged his wife behind the stage at the most recent Willie Nelson Fourth of July picnic. Holly could tell that Melvin was merely proud of accomplishing such a feat without pharmaceutical aid. His talk didn't have even a whiff of perversion.

Holly constantly looked for an out from the Elks, but none appeared. The town was experiencing one of those good times recessions that happen every couple of years in the life of any socially active place. All the scenes had grown stale and the usual rooms tired. Bands didn't tour much this time of year, and those that did usually sucked. If I wasn't working at the Elks, Holly figured, I'd probably be at home anyway, waiting for Netflix to deliver Season Three of Six Feet Under.

One night Lisa called.

"Some of us are heading to the East Side," she said. "There's this blues bar out there full of the sweetest old black men. They wear awesome red hats and call you honey. Plus, they've got a harmonica player who's fucking amazing."

Holly's party sense was tingling.

"When?" she said.

"Friday night."

"Crap," said Holly. "I've got a shift at the Elks on Friday."

Silence on the line. Lisa's voice came back stern. She said, "Holly. The Elks Lodge is over. There's no reason for you to work there anymore. You have to tell them you're quitting."

It's not that easy, Holly thought. You don't know what these people are really like. But she said, "You're right. Of course you're right. I'll do it."

That night, around 9 P.M., Melvin came into the Lodge. Holly had been pouring shots, and Judith had been drinking them, for the last hour. He sat down.

"A round on me," he said. "For everyone."

That meant five people.

"What's the occasion?" Holly said.

"Oh, nothing," Melvin said. "Just a little tete-a-tete in the shower, that's all. I tell you what. Ain't nothing like doin' your business with the same woman for twenty years. And liking it! I'm the luckiest sonofabitch in the world."

Judith raised her glass.

"To Melvin," she said.

"To Melvin," everyone said.

They drank.

"And to my last day on the job," Holly said.

Sly, she thought.

"Pardonnez?" Melvin said.

"My membership expires next month," she said. "I don't want to take up any more of y'all's time. You're probably bored with me."

"Hmm," said Melvin.

"What."

"I don't see how you're going to be able to leave. Judith has decided to abdicate her position on the board, and I've nominated you to take her place."

"Now, Brother Elk," Holly said. "You know I love you. But I don't think . . ."

"Sister Elk," Melvin said. "Did you hear? You've been nominated!"

It was time for the dealer to show her cards.

"Melvin," she said. "Everyone I know has left the Elks. And I'm leaving, too."

"I was afraid you might say that," he said. "So I went ahead and called the state police to tell them about the nine ounces of weed that you've got in the trunk of your car."

"What are you talking about?" she said.

"Also, I told them how you intend to sell the weed at high school graduation parties next weekend. There might even be some middle-school parties in the mix, I told them."

"Goddamn it, Melvin," she said. "This isn't funny. Of *course* I don't have . . ."

Holly looked at Melvin. He wasn't smiling. And this was a guy *who never stopped smiling.* Oh, shit, she thought.

"They should be here in five or so minutes," Melvin said. "And one of two things can happen. They can either find the marijuana and you can go to one of our state's finest women's prisons for the next ten years, or I can tell them I was just blowin' shit up their legs. These guys grew up with me. They'll take anything I dish them as long as I get them high for free after the shift. Whatever else happens, of course, is up to you."

Holly felt the cold knife of fate poking her in the ribs. Suddenly, she knew she wouldn't be going to a blues bar on the East Side with her friends tonight. Or next week either.

She sighed.

"I understand, Brother Elk," she said.

"Joining the Elks Lodge is like adopting a mean and dirty dog," Melvin said. "You owe something to that dog even though he's gonna take a chunk out of your ass once in a while. So now you're going to be an Elk forever. Ain't that right, Judith?"

"That's right, Melvin," said Judith.

Melvin knocked back a shot and slid his glass to Holly for another.

"I tell you what," he said.

Neal Pollack is the author of four books, including the cult classic *The Neal Pollack Anthology of American Literature* and the rock-n-roll novel *Never Mind the Pollacks.* His most recent book is *Alternadad,* a memoir of his early years as a father. The founder of www.offsprung.com, a humor magazine and Web community for parents, Pollack lives in Los Angeles with his wife Regina Allen and their five-year-old son, Elijah.

No! The New Gary Numan

Matt Besser

Sometimes you write a scene that only you "get" but you get it so hard that you want the world to get it, too. I wrote a scene about two Gary Numan fans of different degrees. I slipped it into a pile of otherwise straight-ahead scenes. I knew it would die but I kind of wanted to have that rejection conversation about this one scene. A small percentage of living humans know who Gary Numan is. This scene wasn't rejected in any big dramatic way. It was read and soon forgotten like most mediocre scenes are. The network reaction was polite and diplomatic. "This isn't for our viewers. I get it. I love that song about cars. Our viewers live in Middle America. They're smart, they might know who Gary Numan is, but they don't really care." They were probably right about their viewers, and most viewers (and readers). Many times you have to stand up and fight for a reference. Once when I worked at MTV, I had to fight to use the Beatles as a reference. They said their viewers didn't know the Beatles. "So we'll tell them!" But this scene is not about the Beatles, or Britney Spears, or 50 Cent. This scene is for the Gary Numan fans.

"No! The New Gary Numan" was deemed "too obscure," which is what the scene is about and now obscurity is where it lives. Gary Numan is one of those names where you either think, "Who the fuck is that?" or "Oh, yeah, the 'In Cars' guy."

Int. bar

HOST
Okay, up next at the karaoke we have a regular

here, Tony. And once again we don't have the track
that Tony wants, so he brought his own CD.

TONY

Hello, everyone. How many fans of Gary Numan
do we have out there?

AUDIENCE #1

Yeah! Gary Numan! "Cars"! I live in my car—

TONY

No! Not "Cars"! Not New Wave '80s Gary Numan.
I'm talking about Gary Numan's new stuff. It's
more like Nine Inch Nails.

AUDIENCE #1

Sorry, I didn't know Gary Numan had new stuff.

TONY

Well, then, I guess that makes you ignorant. So
don't yell and scream if you're ignorant.

AUDIENCE #1

I was just trying to show some support. I bet most
people here don't even know who Gary Numan is
at all.

TONY

Well, then, they're ignorant, too. They don't de-
serve to hear Gary Numan.

HOST

Tony, you're not really winning over the crowd.
Why don't you start the song?

TONY

Sure. This is one of my favorite songs off of Gary

Numan's latest release. Although I should point out
that every song on the CD is excellent.

Crowd is getting restless. "Sing the damn song!" He plays the song and
sings over the vocals. It sounds weird.

AUDIENCE #1

Stop singing so we can hear Gary Numan.

TONY

You guys just don't get it! Gary Numan would never
like any of you!

HOST

Okay, give Tony a big hand.

TONY

Wait. I didn't get to sing a full song. Karaoke rules
say you get to sing a full song.

HOST

I am very firm about the karaoke rules.

TONY

I want to sing a Beetles song.

AUDIENCE #2

Yeah, the Beatles! John Lennon, woo hoo!

TONY

No! Not the Beatles from England. I'm talking
about the B E E T L E S, Beetles from Tokyo. It's a
new band that Gary Numan is producing. They
haven't released a CD yet, so I can't sing over that,
but I was able to get my hands on an Emergency
Broadcast Signal, so I'll sing over that.

He sings bad Japanese over the loud squeal.

Matt Besser is a founding member of the Upright Citizens Brigade. He is the creator of the Comedy Central faux debate show *Crossballs*. He has guest starred on *Help Me Help You, Reno 911, The Bernie Mac Show, Frasier,* and in the films *The TV Set, Junebug,* and *Wild Girls Gone.* Matt is the guitarist Dave in the feature film, *Walk Hard,* as well as the evil sheriff in the zombie western film, *Wanted: Undead or Alive,* available on DVD.

In 2008, Matt had some small parts in *Drillbit Taylor* and *Semi-Pro,* and is also writing the Amy Poehler movie for Warner Brothers entitled *Safety First* and is a character in the new Nickelodeon show *Mighty Bee.* At the UCB Theater in L.A., Matt performs in America's Best Comic, a monthly parody of *Last Comic Standing,* and the UCB improv show *Asssscat.*

Matt Besser's MySpace page is at myspace.com/mattbesser.

Ms. Peppermint Twist

Kristen Schaal

Hello, Kristen

    Alas, I'm sorry to say that the editor in chief (*Sunday NY Times Magazine:* The Funny Pages) did not offer to buy and publish your piece. I'm very sorry, since I think it was and is awesome, and I hate the fact that I do not have the final say in these matters.

So I used to work at FAO Schwarz. It was before I got that line in the movie *Norbit*. Yes, that was me saying, "I want to be a ho." And that was you, disappointed.

Before that job, I was a character at FAO Schwarz. FAO casts actors to walk around the store as characters to create an "experience"—an experience that helps them sell toys for almost twice the price of Toys "R" Us. I imagine that the wealthy clientele that frequent FAO Schwarz like to pay more for toys because they need to clean out their money closets. Remove some of that old-dollar clutter. Also, seeing Barbie walk around with Alice in Wonderland is incredibly magical.

The character I auditioned for was an original one they created specifically for the FAO Schweet shop called Ms. Peppermint Twist. Ms. Peppermint Twist was there to assist the customers with whatever candy needs they had, and elevate the candy-buying experience to an even sweeter level. If that's possible.

It's no surprise that I nailed the part. I am Frederick August Otto

Schwarz's wet dream, if he's dreaming of character actors. I look like a fusion of Sandra Bernhardt and Shirley Temple. My voice is like Sarah Vowell lisping on a helium binge. It was only a matter of time before this bittersweet vessel I navigate crashed into a gimmicky toy store.

I had to wear a pink wig, pink sunglasses, striped stockings, and a tutu. I had to wear it for six hours at a time. I had to act like I was into it. It was a nightmare. I would never advocate drinking on the job. Unless your job description was pretending to be happy in a tutu as you guide a fat child between the choice of Swedish Fish or Nerd Rope. (They're both good. It's like choosing between Nietzsche and Sartre. They're both pure sugar.) If that's your job, then I would recommend shotgunning two Icehouse beers prior to clocking in.

I did have some artistic freedom. It was my job to come up with my character's background. I decided that Ms. Peppermint Twist was an orphan. Her mom left her in FAO, very much like Punky Brewster, except this sad girl didn't find her Henry Warnimont. Instead, she stumbled into a giant cotton-candy vat in the basement, which burned her severely and gave her pink hair. Mentally out of sorts from the trauma of the cotton candy accident, she allowed the owners of FAO to enslave her to work in the candy shop for the rest of her days. When customers asked for her story, that's what she told them, following up with: "That's why I'm so tired, because I had to stay up all night making the candy for you and now I have to stand here and watch you buy it." I never got the actual numbers, but it is my belief that candy purchases increased guiltily under Ms. Twist's reign.

Now, I don't want to come off as one of those people who complain about working. I will suck it up and work. And my patchwork résumé will prove that I will take any job. But in order to survive most jobs, you need to have the opportunity to zone out. Your body continues to work but your mind escapes to a place where you can acknowledge your dissatisfaction. Those soul-saving moments to mumble your discontent under your breath as you toil are necessary. Imagine if you saw Ms. Peppermint Twist having that quiet moment in the Schweet shop. It would be unsettling. And so she wasn't allowed any.

But one day it happened. It was slow in the Schweet shop. I had just eaten a handful of chewy peach things and my guard was down as I leaned against the counter. I was reflecting on how I hoped the terrorists didn't destroy America's oldest toy store, melting me down in a sticky pink wig. I was thinking about my coworkers: Barbie, who took private *en pointe* ballet lessons to prepare for the release of Nutcracker Barbie, the Toy Soldier who impregnated Alice in Wonderland (they weren't in Wonderland when it happened, I believe they were in Astoria), and the two cavities I had acquired from the free-candy perk. And that's when one of the managers of FAO happened to be walking by and noticed that my mind was far away from candy.

"Ms. Peppermint Twist, this is not how you sell the candy."

"Oh."

"It's like this!" And he began boisterously welcoming everyone within earshot to the Schweet shop, announcing its goodness, and handing out empty candy bags with such overwhelming joy my cavities started to throb.

"Now, you do it!" He turned to me, after his minute-long demonstration, panting slightly from the exertion.

"I don't know, sir. It's like watching Meryl Streep. I'm never going to be that good. It's pointless to even try. You can't teach an artist how to feel raw emotion. They have to be born that way. I think you should be wearing the wig and the sunglasses, sir."

He didn't agree with my praise. And shortly after I was laid off from the worst job of my life. As for Ms. Peppermint Twist, I can only guess that she is still in that basement, giving a hundred percent to the man.

Kristen Schaal recently won Best Alternative Comedian at the HBO U.S. Comedy Arts Festival in Aspen. She is also the winner of the Andy Kaufman Award hosted by the New York Comedy Festival and the winner for Best

Female Stand-up at the 2006 Nightlife Awards in New York. She is a series regular as Mel on *The Flight of the Conchords* on HBO and is a *Daily Show* special correspondent. In October she was included in *New York* magazine's "Ten Funniest New Yorkers You've Never Heard Of." She co-hosts the bi-weekly variety show *Hot Tub*, which was voted Best Variety Show of 2005 by *Time Out New York*'s readers poll. She co-created a series on the website Super Deluxe called *Penelope: Princess of Pets*, which received a "low brow brilliant" rating in *New York* magazine. Other film and television credits include *Ugly Betty, Freak Show, Cheap Seats, Norbit, Kate and Leopold, Adam and Steve, Delirious, Law & Order: SVU* and *Criminal Intent, The Education of Max Bickford,* Comedy Central's *Contest Searchlight* and *Live at Gotham,* and her own Comedy Central Presents in 2009.

Liarhead

Mike Albo

This is an email (with names concealed) I received after dating some guy for a month or so. Well, maybe it was two weeks, which in a way is a month when you take into consideration the two weeks of post-traumatic obsessing that occurs after some winking liarhead like this sells you down the river.

> Subject: Hey Mikey
> Date: Friday, March 18, 2005 11:22 AM
> From: Someone <aconcealedname@asshole.com>
> To: Mike Albo <shouldichangetogmail@earthlink.net>
> Conversation: Hey Mikey
>
> How was the show in Baltimore? I apologize for not writing sooner about this.

OK, this is three days after he kissed me. We were at this AIDS benefit, free drinks, everyone jubilant and dedicated and political, so that there was this underlayer of morality that made me feel like I wasn't just a cheap selfish thirty-six-year-old who wants to just be in America and in love and oblivious to things. He said he had to go home because he was tired, and I acted like that was cool, and then he leaned over and kissed me for a long enough period of time that I thought that we were finally moving forward after three distant-but-full-of-possibility dates where we went to go see theater together (note: never go to theater again with someone you like, it makes things seem too meaningful and aesthetic) and he made it seem like he was sick of dating guys with perfect muscular bodies like his and wanted to go out with someone quirky and smart that could make him laugh! (Tee hee! That's me! The funny, funny clown of life!) And then a day later I was performing in Baltimore, so of course there was this time after we suddenly made out when I had to leave and dwell over him and his beautiful body, on the Amtrak train, listening to Cat Power.

I haven't really sorted things out in my head as of late.

I have no idea what he is talking about.

Monday and Tuesday were self-medicating evenings.

Oh! I love pills!

I was seeing someone for the last two months and it was a rough last week.

I immediately imagine this person's name to be "Gustavo" or "Pierce" and he has a symmetrical body and a Latina mother, giving him blue eyes and blemishless uniform skin. He and "AConcealed-Name" stand over a bed, and they are the same height, and they are kissing exactly as hotly as they imagine Raging Stallion porn actors kiss when they are doing porn.

"Wow, not only am I getting paid to have sex with someone I am totally attracted to, but I am doing a kind of public service by helping other, uglier and less-fortunate people ejaculate."

Then things came to a head . . .

Lovely. A zit metaphor.

. . . on Monday and that's when I kissed you for selfish reasons.

Aren't kisses always selfish? Aren't we all just desperately tongueing our way outward?

It was nice,

I bet you a million dollars that clause was written after he read it over once and realized he needed to be nicer.

but I'm not sure how much it had to do with you

Get ready.

or just needing that to happen and you were there.

Can you BELIEVE he just said that? I know you are thinking, "Mike, why did you ever even get yourself wrapped up in this guy?" And please understand that he was smart and nice while also having an extremely well-set muscular bod, so when we went out on all those 1950s virginal datesy-dates, I imagined he was finally finding that love and beauty can sometimes descend into our lives. You have to understand the illusion I had created for myself. I don't know who you are reading this, or what it is in your life you can't resist. Maybe imagine this person is a delicious cupcake. Or a gorgeous, flat-stomached personal trainer named Tammi, who has gigantic tits and also went to Stanford and makes you think maybe you will be one of those more regular guys who somehow lands a beauty. Like Billy Joel and Christie Brinkley. But without the divorce.

And I think you are great.

"GREAT"!?

And I need to take some time and learn and work through this.

"By doing a serious abdominal routine, four times a week, eating only water-packed tuna, and really creating washboard definition."

Wednesday night I finally had a chance to just deal with what I was thinking and finally feel some grief and regret.

So, basically I was an emotional laxative.

Anyhow, I think it's best that I don't join you on Monday night for the Drama Department thing.

Why do I always go too far? I don't remember but I can bet you Wednesday night I went home after he made out with me and quickly got online and frenetically invited him to go to this benefit, because I guess I have some kind of dickhead fantasy that I go somewhere and have this really cute smart guy with me like I am Donald Trump.

I don't wish to confuse matters any further than I have already. I hope this makes sense and that you will understand.

To his credit, this is perfectly worded. He places the future of peaceful relations on me, and challenges me to be decorous. That is the worst thing about these kinds of guys (or girls, or cupcakes) that we obsess over. They are always absolutely guiltless and you end up being the craven asshole.

Much Love

This is always the way he signed his emails. Is it just me or is it way too intimate if you are still deciding if you want to live with me forever? Do you at all understand how stupidly invested I was?!

ConcealedName.

Do you Asshole?!

Asshole! Small Business—Try our new resources site!

Mike Albo is a writer and performer who lives and loves in Brooklyn, New York. He is the author of two novels, *Hornito* (HarperCollins) and *The Underminer: The Best Friend Who Casually Destroys Your Life* (Bloomsbury). Check out his website, mikealbo.com for videos, ruminations, his writing archive, and more.

Swim Team 1996

Elizabeth Laime

When I was a sophomore in high school, the coolest thing you could be was a varsity swimmer. Our school was a very athlete-centric establishment. I was already a cheerleader (not as cool as you would think), and a thespian (just as not cool as you would think), but being the social overachiever that I was, I yearned for a spot on the most coveted girls team around . . . The St. Louis Country Day Swim Team.

My best friend, Kendall, was an amazing swimmer, competing in the Junior Olympics every year, and we'd spend summer after summer wrinkled and chlorinated from spending hours on end in her backyard pool. She would "coach" me doing laps, which was more for her entertainment than my benefit, but it had given me enough swimming experience to delude myself into thinking that I should go out for the girls' swim team.

In a feeble attempt to appear accepting of all people, the swimming try-outs consisted of sign-ups where anyone could join the team, followed by a long, painful, and passive-aggressive process of elimination. At the first swim meet, the coach would place the real swimmers in the real races, and then have the others scattered in races throughout the meet, basically to pump up the egos of his prized gals. If you didn't have what it took, they would still technically let you be on the team, but either as an organizer, athletic supporter, or locker room cleaner. There was a tacit understanding that if you were unfortunate enough to have one of these assignments, you should stop showing up to practice and ultimately quit "the team."

To my horror, just minutes before our first meet, the coach announced that I would be swimming in the freestyle 500. This race was not just two, four, or eight laps, but twenty full lengths of our enormous pool. I was swimming alongside the best of the best in the most feared, competitive, and grueling race. Now, it's pretty clear to me in retrospect that the coach had seen my obvious lack of skill during practice and had put me in this race on the very reasonable assumption that I would gracefully decline, thus resigning my position on the team. What he failed to realize was that I, Elizabeth Laime, had a huge sense of false security in my abilities, as well as an enormous desire to be in the cool-kids club. These shallow attributes far outweighed the sensible option of not swimming in the race.

So I wiggled my way into the ridiculously small "speed" swimsuit that I had forced my mom to buy me, crammed my hair into the painful rubber condom hat, and stepped up on that starting block with all the conviction in the world. I looked over at Jill Spitz, the fifth-best swimmer in the state of Missouri, and made it my personal mission to keep up with her stride in the water.

I powered through laps one and two with all of my might—even doing two flip turns at each end. By lap three, the lactic acid in my legs caused them to seize up so that I was left to breaststroke using just my arms to the wall where I paused long enough to watch Jill Spitz in lane one finishing up her entire race. The crowd cheering for her amazing speed gave me the motivation to press onward. The next few laps were a fog of pain, swallowed chlorine water, and embarrassment as all of the other swimmers finished with impressive times. By lap eight I was averaging about five minutes per lap and was the only person swimming in the pool. Lap ten came with a surprising new twist—I vomited twice. Turns out Froot Loops are not the breakfast of champions. Every time I pitifully grabbed ahold of the sidewall between laps, the crowd of about two hundred would rise from their comas to cheer for me—I'm assuming in an attempt to encourage me to quit and stop the misery. Prideful, I could not forfeit to defeat with all those eyes on me, no matter how long it would take.

Forty minutes later, as the people in the stands eagerly looked on for me to finish so they could finally get back to enjoying a real swim meet, I doggy-paddled my last long lap, my muscles quivering just enough to propel me to the end of what surely was the longest swimming race in the history of all time. When I touched that wall, the entire place erupted into celebratory clapping, cheers, and shouts. This endured until, after two pitiable attempts to hoist myself out of the pool, the coach had to come to my lane, lift me out of the water, and carry me back to our team's bench, while the onlookers actually gave me a standing ovation. The emotions I felt were overwhelming. Humiliation, pride, exhilaration, disbelief, and nausea. All wrapped up in one too-small speed swimsuit.

Because of this race, I became a sort of school legend until my heroism was replaced when Hillary Olk scored the tie-breaker goal in the field hockey game against our rival. Ultimately I was allowed to stay on the swim team in the form of the announcer—announcing diving and swimming scores and races during each meet. You might say this was one of those "assignments" that your average self-confident person would pooh-pooh and move on, but if there was one lesson I learned from my racing experience, it was that I do not give up. I became the announcer for not only the girls' swimming and diving meets, but also for the boys' meets and water polo tournaments. In fact, it was in doing this announcing that I found my love for public speaking and ultimately for comedy.

In the end, any form of failure or rejection can be turned into something positive—like finding out more about yourself. I found comedy. And now, here I am: an unemployed comedic actor writing about past failures. See?!

Elizabeth Laime is a writer/performer in New York City. She just finished a run of her one-woman show, *Dear Diary*, at the Upright Citizens Brigade Theatre in New York City and in Los Angeles. She loves to write sketches and short stories. Her pilot, cowritten with Peter Karinen of Pete and Brian, was pitched to Comedy Central and rejected. In her free time she likes to bake and she can also do the Rubik's Cube in under five minutes.

You Are Only in Charge Until They Impeach You

Scott Keneally

Any true fan of David Sedaris knows that *This American Life* can give undiscovered writers a platform from which to launch a successful career. And so a few years back I pored over the show's submission guidelines and considered which pieces from my collection of personal essays were most appropriate. I narrowed it down to five stories and fired them off one at a time. I was hoping that the producers of the show would see something, some brilliance in my self-deprecating, episodic humor that was worthy of orbit in the "Sedarisphere." But each skinny self-addressed stamped envelope that I received in return was stuffed with the same stock rejection letter. It began, "Dear Scott, Thank you for your recent submission to *This American Life*. I'm writing to say that the material you sent isn't quite right for the show ..."

However, on the afternoon that I received my fifth SASE, my heart skipped a few beats when I opened the letter and spotted some real, actual ink on the page. Real actual ink *and* a smiley face! *This could be it!* I thought. *My big break!* I took a deep belly breath and read: "Dear Scott, Thank you for your recent submission ..." It looked suspiciously similar to the other form letters, but then my eyes darted to the handwritten note above the sentence. It read, "Or should I say submission*s.*" The 's' was emphasized and the line was punctuated by a smiley face. *That was rather sinister,* I thought. *Are they mocking me?* Upon reading that I— well, I stopped submitting to *This American Life* altogether. I figured I should give them a few years to forget my name. Or perhaps I took the words of W. C. Fields to heart: "If at first you don't succeed, try again. Then quit. There's no use being a damned fool about it." Here's that final submission.

In fourth grade I wrote a long letter to Ronald Reagan, telling him that, among other things, he was a great man and a "turiffeck presidunt." I informed him that if all went according to plan, in the year 2012, I would be elected President, too. That's when I turned thirty-five and would become eligible to run. A few months later I received a letter and a photograph with a blue signature that wouldn't smear even if you licked your finger and rubbed. I made a mental note to personally write back everyone when I was president, especially future presidents like myself.

It never occurred to me, not even once, that I wouldn't someday be in charge of the United States. This was in part because Mom always told me that I could become *anything* I wanted. Most of my peers wanted to be astronauts or doctors or sports heroes, and while these would surely be fun and important lives to live, nothing caught my imagination quite like the presidency. Helicopters and jets and Secret Service men with guns were all a part of a day's work, although the fame was much of the appeal. The president made important speeches on television and, next to the old Russian man with the brown spot smattered across his forehead, he was the most recognizable face in the world. According to my mother, I was everything the country needed. I was smart and easy on the eyes, with broad shoulders and something called gumption, which sounded pretty good.

For my birthday I received an illustrated book called *The Presidents: From Washington to Reagan.* The cover featured portraits of our first and fortieth presidents, until I cut and pasted my name and class photo over Ronnie's. The book, now titled, *The Presidents: From Washington to Keneally,* was a testament to my destiny. Mom couldn't have been more pleased with my ambition as it made her parenting duties a little *mas facil.* She never had to twist my arm to study, because after all, "Do you really think the people would ever elect someone who skidded by with a B average?"

Absolutely not, and that's why I got As on my report cards. Going to Harvard or Yale was almost a prerequisite to the presidency, and besides, my parents offered to buy me anything at all if I earned an academic scholarship. It made learning fun as every A was one step closer to that new bulletproof Ferrari or a fridge full of soda in my bedroom.

But grades-schmades: I knew that I'd never get ahead if I wasn't well-rounded in other areas. And so in high school I joined lots of clubs, teams, groups, programs, and service organizations. After all, as Mom said, "Nobody wants a president who doesn't care about others." By the end of my junior year, all the tutoring and soup kitchens and As, and my astonishing first place in the New Jersey Physics Olympics egg-drop contest, had paid big dividends. I was selected as a delegate for American Legion Jersey Boys State, a prestigious politics-oriented summer camp.

Each year, kids from every state save Hawaii are plucked from the herd for their "outstanding qualities of leadership, character, scholarship, loyalty, and service to their schools and community." Mom beamed like a solar flare when I broke the news and within seconds was on the phone with her friends. "You won't believe it!"

Mom tracked my movements for everyone she knew. Whether or not they cared was irrelevant as she boasted to this aunt or that friend about what this teacher or that one said about me. No small feat: neither PSAT scores nor report card comments went unnoticed, unreported, unannounced. I know this because she kept me abreast of it all: "So I was telling Aunt Sheila what your English professor said about your latest book report, and boy was she impressed." Sure, I was a little embarrassed by all the attention, but mostly I craved the validation.

According to her, everyone around me saw my star power. Not just she and my father and teachers and friends, but *everyone*, "even people in passing cars." Why else would my school have nominated me for this distinct honor? And best of all, having this on my resumé would surely grease my college application.

The weeklong Boys State summer program was essentially a political camp teaching "future leaders" firsthand about the mechanisms of state, county, and local government. In mock legislative sessions, the kids who were elected to the House or Senate drafted bills, acts, and amendments that were debated and enacted or rejected or debated more. And if at the end of the week I distinguished myself enough to be one of the two kids chosen to go to Boys Nation in Washington, D.C., I'd get to meet Bill Clinton in the flesh. Back in the early '60s, Slick Willy himself was a former Boys Nation pick and had a picture of his brush with JFK to prove it. While I hadn't a clue how to rise to the top of the 750 others, I had set my sights on the Rose Garden.

Throughout that week at Trenton State College, we were packed into a series of dorms named after different towns in New Jersey. We held municipal elections and I ran for mayor of Jackson Township, while other kids ran for other posts like police or fire chief or city clerk or councilman. During the campaign each candidate proposed solutions to the various hypothetical crises facing our city. In my mayoral run I suggested the best way to deal with our prostitution problem was to legalize it in AIDS-safe brothels. I won in a landslide. I also won the next election and the one after that and that, and by the end of the week I was the President of the Senate—the second-highest elected official. I was one of seven kids interviewed for Boys Nation and even privately met with then-Governor Christie Todd Whitman.

As the top dog in the Senate, I moderated the floor of the branch. And I wasn't shy about the perks, swiveling in my leather chair with my legs propped up on a burly oak desk, while the twenty other less-decorated senators sat in plastic folding chairs. I even sent my sergeant-at-arms off to fetch me a Snapple or a snack while I tried looking presidential. While they debated things like the abolition of teachers' tenure, private school vouchers, or handing out free prophylactics in high school, I mostly thought about what I'd say to Bill Clinton next month. I'd joke with him about my letter to Reagan and his own childhood encounter with Kennedy, and I guessed he'd wink and teach me a secret handshake that someday I'd pass along to someone else.

Sometimes the debates were fiery and impassioned, but if anyone got out of line, I flexed my muscles and whacked my gavel. "Order!" I'd bang, bang, bang, like Morse code mapping the frequency of my power trip. I had no problem letting everyone know that "I'm in charge here!" or "It's my show!" There would be no speaking out of turn, or passing notes, or nodding off. I annoyed one kid so much he flung a stack of paper in the air. His insubordination was met with my orders for the sergeant-at-arms to "evacuate him from the premises."

The next morning, the senators rewarded my tyranny in their own special way.

I was impeached.

By an "overwhelming majority."

I was informed that in the program's forty-eight-year history, dating back to 1946, I was the first statesman ever impeached.

And just like in a game of Chutes and Ladders, the route from grace to disgrace was swift and slippery. There would be no brush with Bill, only an airbrush from afar. During the closing ceremony I sat on the stage with the other, less-decorated senators, as the new president gave a speech about his experience as the President of the Senate. Although he had only been in that role for a few hours, luckily he didn't mention the coup. And as two thousand fellow statesmen and parents and others clapped in unison, I contemplated my hubris for a moment.

I couldn't help but think about how quickly power and ego colluded to corrupt me. Within hours of my election to the presidential post, as I rocked in my leather chair and sanctimoniously ordered Snapple and snacks and "Silence!" these kids had already pictured me with the brown spot smattered on my forehead, or perhaps with a pencil-thin moustache over my lip. I took it as a warning sign and quietly drafted new plans for the year 2012.

Fortunately Mom was supportive when those aspirations faded. "In all honesty," she said, "anyone who wants all the pressure of running the world must be nuts." I sighed with relief. I still went to a competitive college and had dreams of success. For a while I entertained the idea of becoming a dentist like my dad or a lawyer like my uncle, before befriending the hippies at school and settling on decidedly less ambitious plans.

When I neared college graduation and told Mom that I was planning on living in a VW bus and touring with Phish, and that I'd support this lifestyle by selling grilled cheese and didgeridoos in the parking lots, it became clear that my mother had lied to me all those years. I couldn't actually become *anything* I wanted.

Scott Keneally writes about the things most people keep to themselves. His stories about chronic bedwetting, crying at Dove self-esteem commercials, sweaty armpits, and his "medical marijuana" prescription have appeared in *Jane, Nylon, Details,* and on scottkeneally.com. When he's not exposing himself, Scott writes treatments for some of the top directors in music videos and commercials. (He's at least partly responsible for Paris Hilton's infamous Carl's Jr. campaign.)

Say My Name

David Rees

My editor knew I was depressed and bored with my career as a cartoonist. I think he got tired of my whining and recommended I try writing a short theater piece. He knew somebody at the Sketchbook theater festival in Chicago. My editor got this fellow to agree to read anything I sent to the festival, with an eye toward producing it. So I let down not *one*, but *two* people when I missed the submission deadline and dropped the following turd in their laps a few days past due. Needless to say, I heard nothing from the theater festival.

MAN and WOMAN are arranging brochures and documents on a folding table, taking them out of boxes and displaying them for passersby (of which there are none). All the characters are wearing blank "Hello, my name is:" badges.

MAN

You were gonna tell me about your friend?

WOMAN

My friend? Oh yeah, my friend.

(Laughs)

This is crazy. My friend is like five months pregnant, and she and her husband have been talking about names for the baby. And her husband has the craziest name picked out—

MAN

Please don't say Thatcher.

WOMAN

He wants to name the baby—

MAN

Cobbler.

WOMAN

Jamesbond.

MAN

James Bond? Their last name is Bond?

WOMAN

    (Looking into the distance; British accent)
Jamesbond.

MAN

Is the father eleven years old? Just name the kid
"Matchbox Car" and be done with it.

WOMAN

You don't understand. He doesn't want to name the
kid James Bond. He wants to name the kid
Jamesbond. It's one word. That's the first name:
Jamesbond.

MAN

What the hell kind of crazy-ass . . . nomenclature
bullshit kind of—their last name isn't even Bond?
What's the point?

WOMAN

He says "Jamesbond" is a nice name. He really just
thinks it sounds pleasant. As a word.

MAN

Jamesbond. So what's their last name?

WOMAN

Goodman.

MAN

(Testing it out)

Jamesbond Goodman.

(In Tarzan voice)

James Bond. Good man.

(British accent)

My name is Goodman. Jamesbond Goodman.

(Shaking his head)

No, no, I'm sorry: That's a total name apocalypse. Because the kid would have to introduce himself like:

(British accent)

"Hello, my name is Goodman. Bond. Jamesbond. Goodman."

WOMAN

I know. The poor kid will never be done saying his name.

MAN

Maybe your friend could give the kid a middle name that somehow explains the rest of the name? Like a secret message about how retarded the dad is?

Long pause while they think of an appropriate name.

MAN (CONT'D)

The middle name should be "Delete." Then, when he says his entire name, it'll sound like an imperative: "Goodman. Bond. Delete. Jamesbond. Goodman." Delete Jamesbond.

WOMAN

A self-destructing name.

MAN

A name you can't say without it actually blowing up.

SECOND MAN walks on stage.

SECOND MAN
(Dramatically)

A name that speaks its own undoing! A name that soils its own underpants! I have such a name!

WOMAN

Good morning.

SECOND MAN

I heard you folks talking about nomenclature name-negators. *Awesome.*

WOMAN
(looking at MAN)

I guess that's what we were talking about . . .

SECOND MAN

Well, I love names, and I love learning names, and I'd love to learn your names.

(To WOMAN, lustily)

I bet your name rings as long and lovely as the Song of Solomon. Am I right?

WOMAN

Actually, my name has nothing to do with the Old Testament. My name is up-to-date and down-to-earth. My name is Destiny's Child.

She offers her hand to SECOND MAN.

SECOND MAN
(Kissing her hand)

May I call you Beyoncé? For your beauty is beyond say-ing.

MAN

(Interrupting, extending hand)

Huh. Well, my name is down-to-earth too. My name is The Rolling Stones. And my middle name is Mick Jagger, Charlie Watts, Keith Richards, and some other old greasy British dope addict I can't remember. I think that's all my middle names, anyway. What's your name?

SECOND MAN
(Laughing, to MAN)

What if my name was Mr. World's Greatest Music Groups? We'd be related!

(Looking sadly at WOMAN)

I don't know about you, though. I don't know if we'd be related, Destiny's Child.

WOMAN

We'd be related. Don't worry about that. History would show us to be related, "Mr. World's Greatest Music Groups," if that is your real name.

SECOND MAN
(to MAN)

I think you should introduce yourself as—

Opening guitar riff from "(I Can't Get No) Satisfaction" should play over loudspeaker at this moment. SECOND MAN's head bobs to the music as MAN looks on, dumbfounded.

SECOND MAN (CONT'D)

It's more dramatic. Why not let people get excited, huh?

MAN

So what's your name? Now you know our names and we don't know your name.

SECOND MAN
(Ignoring the question)

My parents were fascinated with names. For instance, my dad discovered that all American names are nouns, but almost none are verbs. That's crazy, right? My dad discovered that in nineteen-ninety-nine. But ironically, my dad's name was a verb: Carl.

MAN

Carl's not a verb. Do you mean curl? Was your dad's name Curl?

SECOND MAN
(Derisively)

No, my dad's name was not Curl. Because my dad was not a girl.

WOMAN
(Lost in thought)

What verb is carl, then? When you carl, what are you doing?

WOMAN mimes various verb-like actions as she tries to figure out what it would be to "carl."

MAN

Do you mean crawl? Crawl's a verb.

SECOND MAN

Yes! Crawl! Carl! Crawl!

WOMAN

But Carl and crawl aren't the same word.

SECOND MAN

Well, they're not the same *word*, but they're the same *name*, aren't they? Like Dave and David—they're not the same word, but they're the same name.

WOMAN

So your name is David? Dave?

SECOND MAN

No. My dad wanted my name to be a word in the past tense, since my entire life would take place after he named me. So he named me "Afterwards."

MAN

"Afterwards?" That's not a word in the past tense.

SECOND MAN

Oh really? I only see it when I look behind me. . . .

(turns head to look back)
afterwards. Looks like the past tense to me!

MAN

(Sarcastically)
Afterwards, huh? So you're always in the past tense? You're always comin' up behind, like afterwards—

MAN turns his head as SECOND MAN just did, and is shocked to see a DOPPELGANGER OF SECOND MAN standing right behind him.

DOPPELGANGER OF SECOND MAN

HI!!!

MAN

Holy shit!

Lights out while the chorus to "Say My Name" by Destiny's Child is played over the house speakers.

*****

David Rees was working a crummy magazine job when Operation: Enduring Freedom inspired him to make his cartoon *Get Your War On*. The satire about the war on terrorism became an Internet phenomenon. *Get Your War On* now appears in every issue of *Rolling Stone* and as an animated series at www.263.com. David's other comics include *My New Fighting Technique Is Unstoppable* and *My New Filing Technique is Unstoppable*, which appeared every Thursday in the *Guardian* until they dropped it. A Texas theater company called the Rude Mechs adapted *Get Your War On* for the stage, where it ran at the Edinburgh Fringe Festival.

Moby Dick

Jen Kirkman

It was Wednesday and the first eighth-grade dance of the year was forty-eight hours away. I had my hopes set on Alex Hannigan asking me to be his date. I'd never spoken with Alex, unless you counted saying the Pledge of Allegiance at the same time, in homeroom, conversation. Alex was thirteen but he already had five o'clock shadow. He was skinny, like a heroin addict. His jean jacket was vintage, which I thought made him look like a Vietnam vet. And I thought vets were hot. I had a crush on Jim Ignatowski from *Taxi*. Alex never had a pen on him, but always a few guitar picks. He was an underage guitarist who played with twenty-year-old musicians in a real rock band in Boston.

Alex took courses like auto mechanics. The part of me that was ruled by my mother worried for Alex's future, but the teenaged girl in me found the general "fuck you" of tinkering with engines, while others toiled with algebra, to be thrilling. I always wanted to ask Alex if he thought that the episode of *Happy Days* where Fonzie put his bike back together after going blind was realistic or not.

Alex and I had one thing in common: Led Zeppelin. He had written "Zeppelin" in black Magic Marker on his Converse high-tops. My mother outfitted me in sweatshirts with shoulder pads but I knew every lyric to "The Ocean." My sisters, in their haste to get to college, left behind their eight-track collection. I didn't realize what a huge band Zeppelin had been in the 1970s. I thought they were sort of an underground phenomenon, an acquired taste. And the fact that Alex also liked this hidden treasure solidified the fact that we were soul mates.

Now, during this period of having a crush on Alex, I had two best friends. Julie was legally blind and wore big glasses that magnified her eyes from the outside. I think that when God made Julie, he was pushing the limits of "I don't give people more than they can handle," because in addition to being legally blind she also had bucked teeth, frizzy hair, and walked like a duck.

I inherited Julie as a friend because I stuck up for her once when she was getting picked on. Julie's father, the minister, looked up our number in the phone book, called my mother, and said, "We understand your daughter is very Christ-like." We were Catholic but my mom thought that speaking of Jesus outside of church was a little over-the-top, which is why she never said grace before a meal. "God is busy. He doesn't need to hear how thankful we are for every breath and fart." I've always thought that should be embroidered on a pillow.

I liked going to Julie's house because she had the coolest sticker collection and as a Christian she didn't feel like she could keep it all to herself. When I told Julie that I was in love with Alex, she grabbed her rosary beads and said a Hail Mary. Do I need to mention that we'd both never kissed a boy? After our Hail Mary, Julie and I played a game of M.A.S.H., which stood for Mansion, Apartment, Shack, House. It's an intricate game of making lists and figuring out what your future held. I learned that day that I was fated to marry Alex; we'd live in an apartment with no kids and drive a DeLorean. When you don't have kids, you can afford cars like that.

My other best friend at the time was Nicole, who I'd known since sixth grade when she was a dork like me. But after her parents' divorce, Nicole changed her name to Nikki after she discovered Prince's song "Darling Nikki," his ode to a woman who masturbates in hotel lobbies. My friend formerly known as Nicole now wore red lipstick, black eyeliner (on the inside of her eye), and a leather jacket with fringe that was longer than her miniskirt, giving her the appearance of being pantless.

My favorite Led Zeppelin album was *The Song Remains the Same;* my favorite track, "Moby Dick," a tedious ten-minute drum solo. I spent afternoons, lying on my bed, "Moby Dick" blasting through my headphones, staring at my pink flowered wallpaper, blurring my eyes and pretending to be high. During these private moments in my bedroom, daydreaming about Alex, I often paid a visit to a certain private area on my body. I was sure that this too-good-to-be-true feeling that I was giving myself must have been put on Earth by the devil. Oddly enough, it also cleared my sinuses. One afternoon after a particularly mind-blowing session of the devil's work, a brilliant idea came to me. I was going to speak to Alex for the first time by introducing a conversation piece. I was going to buy him a copy of Led Zeppelin's *The Song Remains the Same.*

I washed my hands and headed to the Music Center; where middle-aged musicians who never made it sold records and gave guitar lessons. I spilled my guts to the guy behind the counter. He said, "Man, if a girl had bought me rock and roll when I was growing up, I'd have married her." I started to think about Alex in a whole new light. He needed me. I could change his life. He'd never have to take auto mechanics again.

I walked to school, thinking about how I was going to miss the innocence of my days as a single girl but I also knew that I was ready to be a girlfriend, a wife. I felt weird knowing that I knew Alex's future and he didn't. I guess that's why they say that girls mature faster.

In homeroom, I grabbed my bag and put it on Alex's desk. "Look inside," I said. He took the album. He sleepily said, "I have this record too. You won't like it." He put *The Song Remains the Same* back in my bag, dropped my bag on the floor, and lowered his head to his desk for a nap. I hadn't planned on this. What was I supposed to say now? It took everything I had not to scream at him, "I masturbated to you all afternoon yesterday and this is the thanks I get?"

Nikki came running up to me at my locker after first period. "Do you think Alex Hannigan is cute?" I knew what was happening. Alex was taken aback by my gift. He couldn't handle that moment in homeroom when he was confronted with true destiny. And he sent my best friend to ask me out for him. Nikki interrupted my fantasy, "Alex just asked me to the dance!" I thought this would be a perfect time for God to end my life with an aneurysm, a falling piano, or just old-fashioned spontaneous combustion. I wanted to say to Nicole, "What if Alex likes me, but thinks he can't have me and so just asks out a slut like you because it's easier?"

Friday night, Julie, Jesus, and I stood around at the dance while I watched Nikki and Alex lick each other to "Stairway to Heaven"—even during the fast part. I saw a teacher separating them. Then I saw them come back together and I watched Alex put his hand up Nicole's shirt and then I saw a teacher separating them. I heard Alex say, "Fuck this!" and then I watched a teacher throw them out.

I got a slight chill when Alex said "Fuck" in front of a teacher. I wondered if he'd get in trouble, if his mother would get called and he'd have to spend the rest of his Friday night grounded. One of the chaperones came over to Julie and me and rolled her eyes. She poured herself some punch and leaned back, like a cop taking a break from the beat. She said to us, "Well, there are two losers gone. Good riddance. Now we can get back to having fun, right girls?" Julie agreed. I wanted to hurt Julie, rough her up a little.

I got home from the dance and my mom was waiting up for me. She must have been sitting home all night, having one of those "my-daughter-is-growing-up-because-she's-at-a-dance" moments, because she took me in her arms and said to me, "I am so proud of you. I never have to worry about where you are. You come home after dances and you're not chasing boys." Feeling the safety of my mother's embrace just made me feel more pathetic and un-grown-up. Nicole was probably blowing Alex and I was in my mommy's arms. I tortured myself with a dramatic montage in my mind of Alex and Nikki. That's when I lost it. My mom cradled my head and laughed, "Aww, let it out. These are happy tears." Some things are best left unsaid during a "moment." There's never a good way to say, "Mom, I'm crying because my best friend is dating the long-haired musician that I masturbate to."

Jen Kirkman is a stand-up comedian, actor, and writer who got her start in Boston and New York City and is now a staple on the Los Angeles comedy scene, performing anywhere from the Upright Citizens Brigade Theatre, Largo, and the Hollywood Improv with her storytelling style of stand-up. In February of 2007, Jen released her first comedy album, *Self Help* (available online at aspecialthing.com). She was most recently a cast member on VH1's new sketch show, *Acceptable TV*. Jen has also appeared on Comedy Central's *Premium Blend*, NBC's *Late Friday*, Starz's *Special Sauce*, CBS's *The Late Late Show with Craig Ferguson* and her unique voice has landed her recurring roles on animated shows like Cartoon Network's *Home Movies*, VH1's *Illustrated*, and Current TV's *Supernews*.

The Lifestyle

Jeremy Deutchman

A friend of mine laid it all out, an easy way to make extra money.

"Get this," he said. "I just got paid $50 to have a joke published in *Hustler*. And the thing is," he continued, "the greatest part? I heard it from someone else, and got paid just for *writing it down*."

The thought of being a *Hustler* contributor filled me with an illicit thrill. Through my affiliation, I would join a shadowy underworld of Mafia hit men and bisexual strippers, a nice change from my usual crowd. I would be able to reference my "work with *Hustler*" at dinner parties and in the conversations I sometimes struck up with supermarket baggers. And I would be able to say things like, "Go ahead and spend my blood money," anytime my wife Michelle went to Nordstrom. It would be hard to mount a case against the skin trade when peddled flesh was keeping us in sling backs and mules.

Through a connection, my friend offered to get me a "starter kit" from LFP, the company that published *Hustler*. The magazine came bundled together with a collection of other LFP blockbusters, including *Barely Legal, Taboo, Asian Fever,* and *Busty Beauties,* as well as a guide that detailed the "do's" and "don'ts" of pornography writing. After a quick review of the contents, I decided the most promising avenue of approach was the section called "Hot Letters." The magazine asked for a couple hundred words about my "personal sexperiences," which on the surface seemed easy enough. Based on the examples I saw, it looked like all I had to do was make as many references as possible to my "throbbing pole" and my partner's "tight quim," and in a matter of weeks I'd have amassed enough for a vacation in Tuscany.

The only problem was, I was terrible. I had always prided myself on being creative, but in the sexperience department I was coming up dry. My perfectionism didn't help, either; I kept telling myself my readers weren't going to care that I'd used "oozing pussy juice" in two consecutive sentences, but I knew I could do better.

I called my *Hustler* friend looking for inspiration. "I've got just the thing," he said. "A friend of mine just finished working on a documentary about swingers. Called *The Lifestyle*. It's kind of out there, but should give you something to work with."

I had stayed home from work with a sore throat, which gave me the perfect opportunity to continue my research. I ran out and picked up the movie. Sure enough, it was an exploration of swinging, the swapping of sex partners that participants called The Lifestyle. These were ordinary middle-aged couples, many of them small town and suburb dwellers who were conservative in everything but their preference for group sex and their use of bronze penis statues as part of their interior design scheme.

The film was eye-opening and a little disturbing. I was just at the part where a pair of senior citizens were making love on a weightless swing when Michelle walked in from her day at work.

She dropped her bag where she stood. "I guess your throat's feeling better." Her tone managed to convey both surprise and a weary resignation, as though she should have expected this all along.

I considered things from her perspective—she'd left that morning as I was drinking lemon tea and reading *The New Yorker;* less than ten hours later I was scanning *Asian Fever* and watching a couple of horned-up seventy-five-year-olds do the missionary position in a zero-gravity harness. I could see how the situation might be confusing.

"Hold on," I said, pausing the video. "I know it looks weird, but this is actually important field research." I tried to explain my plan, that we were basically just a few orgasms away from a new Lexus, but I could tell it wasn't resonating with her.

I tried a different tack. "Isn't this what couples do?" I asked. "Support each other's dreams?"

"Not if the dreams involve senior citizens fucking," she said. I had to admit she had a point.

A few nights later, our new neighbors invited us over for a glass of wine. I had complained to Michelle that we hardly knew them, and from the little we did know we had nothing in common. She waved off my concern with a casual, "Just try to be normal," which seemed both challenging and unfair.

Two hours in, things were going well, largely because Michelle was making all the conversation and I was drinking all the wine. It seemed like a perfect arrangement, until Michelle got up to use the bathroom.

"So, how do you guys like living here?" I asked. They had recently moved into the apartment across the hall.

"It's neat," said Grace, a relentlessly upbeat, blonde, five-foot-eleven giantess who doubled as a registered nurse.

"Sure is," said Craig, her strapping husband-with-an-MBA.

Even in the artificial glare of cheap halogen lights, their cheeks glowed with the healthy all-American flush of private yachts and white-wine spritzers. Compared to the two of them, Michelle and I looked like we had just gotten off a boat from the Ukraine.

One question, and I was already out of conversation. I looked around the apartment and grabbed for some more.

"What do you think about the fireplace?" I asked.

I immediately felt the full weight of my conversational lameness. Our fireplaces were standard apartment issue, the kind that burned gas and turned off and on with the flick of a switch. There was nothing remarkable about them.

"Well, I for one think it's pretty cool," said Grace, coming to my rescue. I loved Grace.

"Yeah," echoed Craig, jumping onto the bandwagon. "Reminds me of my bachelor days." I wasn't entirely sure I wanted to know about Craig's premarital gas-fireplace exploits, but I appreciated the effort.

Still no sign of Michelle. How long did it take someone to pee? I knew it could be awhile, especially if she found a scale in the bathroom. Michelle was always open to the possibility that she would weigh less at other people's houses. Brushing by me on her way back from freshening up, she'd often whisper, "Can you see if it's accurate?" like she was on a mission to calibrate every scale in West Los Angeles.

I had to face facts: She had temporarily abandoned me, and I was on my own. The key was not to panic, to find an easily relatable subject that would make the chitchat something everyone could enjoy.

"Speaking of 'bachelor days,' I just saw this crazy movie I think you guys would really like," I said to two people I had basically met an hour before.

"Really?" said Craig. "That's awesome—We love movies! What's it about?"

"It's about swingers," I said, expecting a nod of recognition but eliciting only blank stares. Jesus, did I have to do all the heavy lifting? "You know, those couples who go to parties and have group sex."

"Excuse me?" said Grace, her high-pitched chirp sounding strangled.

"Yeah," I said. I knew I should probably stop, but was afraid of slowing our momentum just as it was hitting its stride. "It's pretty wild. During the day they're like stockbrokers and doctors or whatever, but at night they get together in these party houses where some of the rooms are like 100% bed and the ceilings are all mirrored and they become totally insatiable."

If instead of sparking lively discussion, my intention had been to kill it dead without hope of resuscitation, I had hit the mark. By the time I finished, the two of them were looking at me like I had just spit up the Lindbergh baby. Grace in particular looked completely shocked. Craig seemed more confused, until a light of comprehension spread slowly across his face.

"Honey," he said, turning to his wife, "I think we're being propositioned."

My face was instantly hot. We had obviously had some kind of misunderstanding. I was trying to be friendly, but not *that* friendly. And did he think I was some kind of whore? If I had been a swinger, I would like to think that I'd have some integrity.

Michelle walked back into the room. "So what'd I miss?" she asked, settling down next to me on the couch.

"Oh, not much," I said offhandedly. "I was actually telling them about that movie I saw the other day."

"Which one?" she asked sharply, her tone a warning I'd better mean something that wasn't known for its single-camera close-ups of a vagina.

"You know, *The Lifestyle.*"

"Why would you do that, Jer?" she asked a little too brightly, with a look that would have withered AstroTurf.

As I struggled to find an answer, Craig stepped in.

"It's okay," he said. He smiled and even blushed a little. "I'm actually sort of flattered." He turned to Grace. "I don't know, babe—what do you think?"

Terrific. I had forgotten to add "group sex encounter with male neighbor" to the list of life experiences I would be okay with skipping.

"I think I've expressed myself badly," I said. "I didn't mean to suggest . . ." I trailed off, at a loss, and glanced over at Michelle, who looked like she wanted to stick her head in a blender.

"Aw, forget about it," Craig said good-naturedly. "We'll pretend it never happened." He raised his glass and winked at Michelle.

A few minutes later, it was over. After negotiating an awkward series of goodbye hugs, we were out the door.

"Well, that was nice," I said, as we headed back to our place.

Michelle just looked at me and rolled her eyes.

"I'm going to bed," she said. "And look, I don't want to interfere with your career development or whatever. But how about you do me a favor and take *Teen Pussy* off the coffee table before my parents come over for brunch tomorrow?"

It didn't seem like an unreasonable request.

Jeremy Deutchman's essays and opinion pieces have appeared in such publications as the *Los Angeles Daily News*, *The Philadelphia Inquirer*, and *Tikkun* magazine. He is the co-author of *Whiplash! America's Most Frivolous Lawsuits* (Andrews McMeel Publishing). Jeremy lives with his wife in Santa Monica, California.

Cantor D.

Jackie Cohen

Dear Miss Cohen,

I regret to inform you that I am unable to accept you into Congregation Adath Jeshurun's choir. As founder and director of said choir, I feel it is my duty to accept only the finest voices that our suburban synagogue has to offer. Unfortunately, as you demonstrated in the audition with your rendition of "Dreidel, Dreidel," you are unable to carry, what we in the music business call, "a tune."

In the small chance that your voice and sense of musicality improve in a year's time, I would be happy to grant you the opportunity to re-audition for the choir.

I wish you luck in not bringing your family shame in the years to come.

Sincerely,

Cantor D.

Back when I was blissfully unaware of my limitations as a singer, my mother dragged me to what I thought was the first day of choir *practice* at our synagogue, but what we later learned was in fact an *audition*. Regardless of what it was, I didn't want to go. I hated performing in front of people, and I especially resented the fact that my mother was forcing me into Jewish extracurricular activities. But, like a good Jewish little girl, off to choir "practice" I went. Needless to say, I didn't have what it took to impress the cantor and win a prestigious spot among the talented little Jewish children of Elkins Park, Pennsylvania. Yes, I was rejected from choir. I was five years old.

Luckily for me, I was thrilled to be rejected. I had no idea that I couldn't carry a tune. In fact, I didn't know what carrying a tune even meant. I thought singing was singing. I didn't think one could be bad or good at it. Like talking. But, as I learned from Cantor D., I was bad at it, and happily so—at least for the time being—because it meant: Woohoo! No choir practice! Ever! Maybe subconsciously I knew I wasn't a very good singer, which could explain my relief to learn I was rejected from the choir. Or maybe it was that I just didn't like performing in front of people in the first place. Whatever my reason, it was only reinforced by my new label as "synagogue choir reject." I was now, at age five, officially a bad singer.

The worst part of being rejected from the choir was my mother's wrath against the cantor. How dare he not let her daughter sing her little Jewish heart out? I didn't understand my mother's desire for me to stand with a group of other five- to seven-year-olds and belt out "Shalom Aleichem" to camera-wielding parents. As far as I was concerned, the cantor was doing my potential audience a service by *not allowing* me to sing in public. The problem was, however, he had squashed my interest in being able to sing at all—whether in public or in the shower (or in a public shower).

The cantor had caused me quite a dilemma. Knowing I had a bad voice, I was embarrassed to sing anywhere, and yet, I loved music. A few years after the choir debacle (and yes, according to my mother, it was a debacle), I found myself in the backseat of a car with a friend from my soccer team (soccer was my activity of choice; school plays were out of the question) when "Broken Wings" by Mr. Mister came on the radio. The first thing I thought was "Omigod, I love this song" ('cause, um, who doesn't?). The second, "I must sing along." And so I sang. Loud. Yes, I *will* "take these broken wings and learn to fly again and learn to live so free!" Thanks for the suggestion, Mr. Mister! But, when the second verse came along and I didn't know the words, I took the opportunity to catch my breath and rest my voice in preparation for the next chorus. In this moment of silence as I was pondering the meaning of broken wings (clearly, they represented my voice) and Mr. Mister's first name, my friend turned to me and asked, "Are you *trying* to sing?" Ouch. My heart sank. Trying? I *was* singing . . . "No. Why would I ever do a thing like that—ever again?" And so, my attempt at singing, even with the radio turned way up, was once again crushed. My voice had failed me again and this time I hadn't even auditioned.

Was it really that bad? I was too self-conscious to ask anyone, for surely in order to determine the quality of my voice, the person in question would have to hear it. The more self-conscious I became about my singing voice, the worse it got, I feared. Every time I was required to sing (at the Jewish day school I attended there was way too much required singing) I would get nervous. The more nervous I got, the shakier and more off-key my voice became. It was a vicious voice cycle. A "voicious" cycle, if you will. Would it ever end? Was there any way that my voice could actually one day improve, magically? ('Cause there was no way I was actually going to practice singing. That would require . . . singing.) When a good song would come on my mix-tape (and they were all good, because it was *my* mix-tape) what was I to do? Sing and offend the people around me? Or purse my lips and try to get the same satisfaction by singing in my head, rather than out loud? Have you ever tried it? It's like holding in a sneeze or a fart. Painful.

The solution to my problem came from an unexpected source: Rosie O'Donnell. I remember seeing her on TV, talking to an actress who admitted to Rosie that she had a bad voice. Rosie told her that it doesn't matter if you have a bad voice, as long as you sing with gusto. I don't usually make a habit of taking anything Rosie O'Donnell says to heart, but when she told that actress to sing with gusto, a whole new world opened up to me. From then on, I would also sing with gusto! I would embrace my bad voice. If only Rosie had been there with me at the choir audition. If only she had been there in the car when Mr. Mister came on. I would have had the courage to tell my friend, "Not only am I trying to sing, I *am* singing . . . bitch."

My rise back into the world of singing started slowly. I sang along to the radio in front of friends. I took an improv comedy class where I had to sing in front of strangers—a big feat for me. As I tested the water one song at a time, I realize that not only did no one care whether I could sing or not, but also that I didn't care what other people thought. (This proved truest when I would find myself drunk and singing Prince's "Let's Go Crazy" at late-night karaoke sessions with coworkers. Key word: drunk.) I still know my limits though. While I will sing Prince or Bon Jovi during karaoke, I still draw the line at the likes of Billie Holiday or Eminem (it's really hard to rap!).

I knew I was fully recovered from Cantor D.'s rejection when I agreed to go with a friend to sing karaoke completely sober, in the middle of the day. After the first time of sober karaoke, I was hooked. During a period of unemployment, my friend and I would regularly get a two-person room at an authentic Japanese karaoke bar in Manhattan and take turns singing every other song, for three-hour stretches at a time. If there's anything more fun than that, please inform me. I had arrived. Singing had actually become enjoyable for me, rather than torturous.

In a world where *American Idol* is the top-rated show week after week, I've come to terms with the fact that I'll never be Kelly Clarkson, or even Sanjaya. Simon Cowell would rip me a new one in the first episode. Thanks to Cantor D., I know there's plenty of room for improvement. The year after being rejected from the choir, my mother brought my younger brother, who was then old enough, and I back to Congregation Adath Jeshurun to audition (she was determined, even if I wasn't). After both of us once again reluctantly sang for Cantor D., the cantor pulled my mother aside and said, "This year I can lower my standards for your daughter, but I cannot lower them enough to let your son in." After another hour of my mom yelling at the cantor, we were officially finished with choirs and organized singing forever. "Happy Birthday" is as close as we get. My voice hasn't improved much since Cantor D.'s choir audition. I still can't sing for shit, but at least I can sing with gusto.

Jackie Cohen has been a writer and producer for various Viacom networks, including VH1, Comedy Central, and Nick at Nite. She has also written for the Oxygen Network, FreshYarn, and the New York City Commissioner to the U.N. (naturally).

Pseudo Phone Sex with a Comedy Central Executive

Tom McCaffrey

In 2003 I was getting ready to perform on Comedy Central for the first time on the now-defunct standup show *Premium Blend*. It was a pretty big deal to me and I was very psyched and nervous. I was supposed to do a ten-minute set. After months of working and reworking my set, I got a call from the Standards and Practices office at Comedy Central. Standards and Practices are the people who tell you what you can and cannot say on their network. I had given them a tape of the set I was planning to perform. It was a set I had been doing for the last four months, which I had perfected. The following is a true (and typical) transcript of that phone call:

> Comedy Central: Hey, Tom, this is Diane over at Comedy Central. How are you?
>
> Tom: I'm good. How are you?
>
> Comedy Central: Great. Listen I watched your tape and there are a few problems.
>
> Tom: Problems? Oh?
>
> Comedy Central: Yeah, listen, you can't do that joke about the gay dream.

I have this joke where I'm talking about a friend of mine who asks me to interpret a dream and it's so obviously a gay dream but I don't feel comfortable telling him that. He's like, "Hey, what do you think of this dream? I'm in the forest and I'm making out with ten hot guys and then they all start licking my balls." And I say, "Ahhh . . . you're gonna get a job promotion."

Comedy Central: You can't say "licking my balls."

Tom: What do you mean?

Comedy Central: You can't say "licking my balls" on the show.

I was sort of surprised although I should not have been. I mean, looking back, how did I ever think that I would be able to say "licking my balls" on TV?

Comedy Central: Look, we discussed it and you can say "They were all touching my private area."

Tom: Private area?

That's like if they told the producers of There's Something About Mary, "Listen, you can't have him get his penis caught in his zipper. Have him sprain his pinky toe." It took the meat out of the joke, so to speak.

Tom: How about "licking my penis"?

Comedy Central: No. You can't say "licking my penis."

Tom: "Sucking my shaft"?

Comedy Central: No. You could say "stroking my genitals."

Tom: Well, how about "They were tonguing my nuts"?

Comedy Central: No. You absolutely cannot say "tonguing your nuts."

Tom: I watched the show last season and a girl said she gave a guy a handjob. How come I can't say licking my penis?

Comedy Central: Well, I didn't see that episode but I think licking your penis is worse than giving a handjob.

Tom: Worse?

Comedy Central: How about "stroking my butt"?

Then it hit me: I am on the phone with an executive from Comedy Central and I'm saying things that I wouldn't say to a prostitute. I told her that I would just scrap the joke altogether. It just wouldn't work if it had to be toned down so much. She apologized and hung up. When the show aired three months later, three of my entire bits were cut out. One of them was the joke that I had replaced the gay dream with. So ultimately it didn't even matter.

After the taping I met the Standards and Practices woman in person. She wasn't at all my type but I could tell that she was totally into me.

In 1996 **Tom McCaffrey** studied acting at the William Esper Studio and in 1999 he began his career in stand-up comedy in Los Angeles. In 2002 he moved back to New York City and in 2003 he was chosen from thousands of tape submissions to compete in Comedy Central's Laugh Riots national stand-up competition. He won the New York semifinals and was flown out to Los Angeles to compete in the finals, where he placed Third Runner-up. Later that same year he appeared on Comedy Central's *Premium Blend*. In 2004 he appeared on Comedy Central's *Shorties Watchin' Shorties* alongside such comics as Janeane Garofalo and Jim Gaffigan. That same year Comedy Central chose him as one of their Fresh Faces of Comedy, which entailed him shooting three separate national commercial TV spots. In 2005 he was tapped by Comedy Central again to host their *Secret Stash* movie for three straight weeks. He was then asked to perform on the *Invite Them Up* CD/DVD compilation produced by Comedy Central Records. A review of the CD in *Punchline Magazine* singled out Tom's set as one of the standout performances. He has also appeared on the VH1 show *All Access*. He has written for *The Onion*, which once called him "consistently funny."

Factors Not Taken into Account When Decorating Pizzeria Walls Liberally with Autographed Headshots in the 1980s

Liz Koe

Contrary to popular belief and the strong sense of disappointment you will most likely develop in the course of reading this, the following piece was never actually rejected. That is to say, not in its entirety. The central premise behind it was pitched as an idea for a comedic Web video. At the time, the idea was summarily dismissed. What you see before you today is the product of one individual's dubious choice to embrace a rejected idea, throw caution and sound advice to the wind, and invest in that idea far more time and energy than could be considered advisable. You might think that this is some kind of an epic story of triumph in which the shining protagonist proves her rejectors wrong. This would be a kind but erroneous assumption. Instead, it's just a simple lesson about how to thrive in life by consistently creating an environment of lowered expectations for each of your endeavors.

The following is a series of emails sent by James Potts to an unmonitored email account created in 2001 by Gino Petrazelli, then-manager of Famous Ray's Pizzeria.

From: James Potts <LilJamiefan309@hotmail.com>
To: <famousrays@hotmail.com>
Sent: Sunday, January 7, 2007 10:37:59 PM
Subject: Mama Mia! Whatta Pizza!

Dear Famous Ray's,

Found this email address on your trifold take-out menu and I just wanted to drop you a line to say GREAT SLICES! Your pizza is still fantastic after all these years. The stuff really holds up.

On another note—I thought I should alert you to the fact that one of the autographed headshots on your wall seems to have accidentally fallen off. Oops! You guys are so busy painstakingly breading chicken cutlets for your delicious parmigiana and carving prosciutto like lace for your legendary antipasti that you probably hadn't even noticed! I didn't want to step on anyone's toes or tell you guys how to do your job or anything, so I thought this friendly email would be best.

Thanks!

Jim

From: James Potts <LilJamiefan309@hotmail.com>
To: <famousrays@hotmail.com>
Sent: Wednesday, January 17, 2007 2:07:09 PM
Subject: Pizza at its Best, only at Ray's

Dear Famous Ray's,

A quick note to say "Keep up'a the great'a work'a!" I had your mussels marinara today, and believe me when I say they were absolutely "Bellissimo!" (I'm kissing my fingers while saying this, btw.)

Also, just a heads up, but that headshot is still missing. I realized in my last note I didn't explicitly indicate its exact location, so you guys must have looked for it and thought, "What the!? Is this guy crazy or something? I don't see any autographed photo missing! Fahgettaboutit!"

The empty space can be found right in between the photos of Sinbad and Tara Lipinski. If you were to stand in front of the cash register, the spot would be just above the bowl always piled high with your savory garlic knots that sits on the glass display case that houses your mouthwatering calzones!

Keep up the great pizza-making!

Jim

From: James Potts <LilJamiefan309@hotmail.com>
To: <famousrays@hotmail.com>
Sent: Monday, January 29, 2007 11:07:09 PM
Subject: Famous indeed!

Dear Famous Ray's,

Here's just a little word from a local pizza lover to his favorite pizza restaurant: YOUR PIES ARE TO DIES FOR! Had a great slice tonight with mushrooms so fresh—I can't believe they're actually fungi!

Also, on the headshot, I realized I never told you which one it was exactly so you probably didn't know what to look for. It's actually—and it embarrasses me a little to admit this—mine! The headshot was taken when I was thirteen and starring in 1985's top-rated sitcom *Lil' Jamie* in the title role. It has a personalized note on it, too, in a felt-tipped marker that says, "Finest slices in town! All the Best, Lil' Jamie."

So, I hope that helps!

Your friend,

Jim (formerly, "Lil' Jamie" of *Lil' Jamie*)

From: James Potts <LilJamiefan309@hotmail.com>
To: <famousrays@hotmail.com>
Sent: Wednesday, January 30, 2007 6:37:00 PM
Subject: No subject

Ray's,

Noticed the headshot must be still stuck between the register and the wall. You guys should really fix that because, honestly, the markedly cleaner spot on the exposed brick where the acrylic frame used to hang just kind of makes it seem like Ray's maintenance staff isn't up to snuff if you know what I mean!

Just kidding! You guys run a tight AND very sanitary ship over there. Hahaha. No, but you really should hang it back up though.

Jim

From: James Potts <LilJamiefan309@hotmail.com>
To: <famousrays@hotmail.com>
Sent: Thursday, January 31, 2007 3:20:24 PM
Subject: An observation

Noticed that the lunchtime "crowd" was a little sparse today. It's always best to avoid speculation, but I wonder why business is so bad? As a member of your esteemed cavalcade of celebrity sponsors, I can't imagine why! Don't worry—I don't expect any special treatment (like buy-one-get-one slices or complimentary refills on fountain soda) despite having served as a pizza ambassador for you for the last twenty years. My head-shot in its key position above the eye-line of the garlic knots is basically a great voucher for the quality of your product. It's a role I'm ever happy to serve.

You should really fish out that headshot. I tried to gauge the size of the gap between the counter and the wall and it is pretty small—about two inches I think. But, I could help move the register next time I'm in, in case that's something you might be interested in.

Jim

From: James Potts <LilJamiefan309@hotmail.com>
To: <famousrays@hotmail.com>
Sent: Thursday, January 31, 2007 11:59:09 PM
Subject: Duh!

Oh, I just feel silly! I just realized that maybe the nail is just crooked! Maybe all these times you've been putting it back up and it's just been falling back down into the crevice between the counter and the brick wall. Maybe you should push the register up against the wall? I can bring a ham-mer and the bendless heavy-duty nails I just picked up at the hardware store the next time I'm in.

Jamie

From: James Potts <LilJamiefan309@hotmail.com>
To: <famousrays@hotmail.com>
Sent: Friday, February 1, 2007 12:01:09 PM
Subject: Official Declaration of Limitation of Liability, Dated January 24, 2007

(A notarized hard copy of the following email correspondence will be de-livered by the United States Postal Service with request of delivery receipt within 3–5 business days.)

To the Management Team of Famous Ray's:

It has recently come to my attention that a certain autographed head-shot has been *DELIBERATELY* removed from the 63rd street Famous Ray's Pizzeria. The headshot in question is an 8½" by 11" glossy of the famed '80s sitcom phenom "Lil' Jamie" Potts. This letter is to officially decline all liability for any financial losses your establishment may incur as a result of removing this piece of marketing material. The party named below takes no responsibility for decline in pizza pie sales that will result from this fis-cally reckless action.

The party named below originally thought the headshot had acciden-tally fallen from its rightful place on the celebrity wall of Famous Ray's. The party named below then went through a phase in which he convinced himself that the photo had been only temporarily removed for a good cleaning—a theory that made sense as over the years instances of splat-tered marinara had added a series of new "birth marks" to Lil' Jamie's oth-erwise youthful and unblemished face. However, upon visiting the establishment this afternoon and speaking to Angel Ramos, an employee, the party named below discovered that the photo was purposefully re-moved supposedly due to frequent customer questions (example cited: "WHO the hell is that?"), customer commentary (examples cited: "That show blew and the sound of that kid's grating voice was worse than nails on a chalk board/a squeaky screen door/the sound of my grandfather clip-ping his toe nails on the other side of the wall of my childhood bed-room/the midnight shrieks of street cat rapings" and so on), and customer requests (example cited: "God that kid's creepy, can you please take that down? I don't like the way he's looking at me.").

To illustrate and forecast the extent of the inevitable damages, I refer to Episode 107 of *LIL' JAMIE,* which aired on March 15, 1985 (DVD-R trans-ferred from original VHS recording can be furnished upon request). After the opening credit sequence (montage of Lil' Jamie moments from previ-ous seasons showing his playful but lovable nature), the episode begins with Lil' Jamie's mother trying to wake Lil' Jamie for a day at school. But the wily Lil' Jamie, intent on his usual shenanigans, feigns illness by comi-cally mimicking a whooping cough and swaying dizzily about his rocket-ship adorned bedroom and exclaiming, "I don't feel so good, Mommy." At one point, Lil' Jamie tries to brush his hair with his saddle shoe and put his comb on his foot. This memorable moment was ad-libbed by the actor, because he had once heard that fever caused delirium. Ultimately, Lil' Jamie's parents give in and let him stay home by himself. He commits all sorts of antics while they are gone, including making a horrible mess of the kitchen with a comically oversized bag of flour and letting his cat Sheba out on the fire escape while trying to rig a wire hanger in just the right way to get the nudie channel. His parents come home and find the house trashed and realize their precious Siamese has vanished. Lil' Jamie, an incredible actor—a real actor amongst actors, regardless of his age—begins to cry honest to God tears at his loss. Then, the doorbell rings and the sassy black neighbor comes in, visibly angry. He sternly tells Lil' Jamie that the cat was darting across the street and jumped out in front of his Cadillac Seville. Jamie shudders, "No! Sheba! It's all my fault." The neighbor goes into the hallway and comes back with Sheba in his arms and says, "Next time, you better eat them apples!" The laughter swells and the shot goes in close on Lil' Jamie, who mugs for the camera, winks, and says, "I sure will, Mr. Jones! I sure will!"

The moral of this story and how it pertains specifically to the impending doom poised to befall Famous Ray's is abundantly clear. The headshot-Sheba analogy is a solid one. The only difference being that friendly Mr. Jones does not live next door but soon Mr. Domino's or Mr. Papa John's will.

On a personal note, the party named below wants to stress that while there are grounds for a lawsuit, he does not plan to press charges. The pain and suffering caused by the removal of the headshot and the fact that he now has nowhere to take his visiting mother out to dinner that could possibly validate his existence as a human being in the same way as a headshot hung above the Famous Ray's cash register would, will be suffered in silence.

In conclusion, the party named below officially severs all ties with Famous Ray's and will ne'er dine in or accept delivery from said establishment ever again. Instead, he will patronize other bustling local businesses whose success is due in no small part to the presence of a Lil' Jamie auto-graphed headshot hung in a prominent location. (Two such enterprises that will continue to benefit financially from these photos include a Halal concern on 72nd Street called Haji Baba's and Pete's Salt Water Fish Depot on 17th.)

Sincerely,

James L. Potts

Liz Koe writes sketch comedy in New York City and is a contributor to *The Onion* News Network. Having arrived on earth via New Jersey, she considers herself predestined to a lifetime rife with uniquely painful and humiliating rejections. She rejects herself on a daily basis.

Various Early Rejections

Colin Jost

> These are fake anecdotes I submitted to the "Life's Like That" section of *Reader's Digest* while I was in college. They were supposed to be true stories, but they paid like $200 and my real life wasn't that interesting. So I made them up. They were all wisely rejected.

One fall afternoon, my neighbor was telling me how cute the squirrels outside his house looked. "I love the way squirrels build up fat for the long winter," he said. "I wonder where they find enough food to get that chubby?" The next day, when my neighbor discovered a family of squirrels had been living in his attic and eating the food he had in storage, "cute" was not the adjective he used to describe his furry friends.

My dad coaches a high school lacrosse team, and he was trying to decide how many players to cut before the next game. "I think I'm only going to dress thirty players for the rest of the season," he resolved. My brother replied: "I suppose the rest will have to dress themselves."

My ex-wife was getting remarried, so I decided to attend the wedding as a sign of friendship. Since the ceremony was right around Easter, I drove down to her hometown a few days early to avoid the holiday traffic and enjoy the extra vacation.

I was driving a little too fast through her neighborhood, and a policeman pulled me over. Hoping to avoid a ticket, I made up a quick excuse: "I'm late for a meeting with my ex-wife, officer. She's annoying enough as it is, so I wanted to keep her happy, you know?" "I *should* know," he said after examining my license. "I'm the guy she's gonna marry."

For my senior prom, I really wanted to wear a very tight, low-cut evening gown I recently saw at the mall. But I knew my father would have problems with his little baby girl going to the prom in a revealing dress. So I planned to describe my outfit in the nicest way possible. I would tell him it was a lovely strapless evening gown and very sensible.

When I approached my father, though, I quickly went into a panic. Glaring at me, he asked, "So, what are you wearing exactly?" "A gownless evening strap and it's very sensual," I blurted out. Needless to say, I didn't get to wear it.

The Life of a Man

I submitted this poem to *The New Yorker* in my junior year of high school. For some insane reason, they rejected it. In fact, they mailed it back to me *cut up into pieces* with a note that said something like "*The New Yorker* has no use for your materials at this juncture." That's an extremely thorough rejection. Yet, it deserved worse.

Not once did he look back upon his life in disgust
Not once did he wish for someone to sweep him away to the
    next adventure
Not once did he see in another the hope for a lifetime
Not once did his dream dry up and crumble
Not once did he venture into the world of endless colors
Not once did the artist dash his hopes with an errant brush.

Only once did he feel a kiss touch his soul
Only once did a star catch his eye on a wintry eve

Only once did the fire lose control
Only once did he lose his love forever.

Never did her tears touch the ground
He caught every one
Never did her skin graze the dirt
His loving arms sealed her tight
Never did he love another
Never did another love him
Never did he laugh or mourn
Never did he sing or scorn

Never did he leave the night
Alone, he remained 'til death

2/15/99

Side Effects

This was my submission for an anti-smoking essay competition in high school. The winner received a $1000 scholarship for college. All the biographical and anecdotal information is 100% false. No one in my family smokes. None of my friends in high school smoked. I never "educated my peers" about smoking. It's all lies. Thankfully, the essay is terrible in addition to being fraudulent, so I didn't win the scholarship.

Thick, rank clouds of haze rising from my Uncle Charlie's cigar at his weekly bridge game. Noxious tobacco odors infecting my clothes and penetrating every last crevice of my uncle's basement. When he bends over to show me his cards, I can only turn away in disgust, not fully comprehending why such a great uncle would want to throw his lungs, and ultimately, his life, away.

My old friend Tim at age thirteen: handsome, athletic, and popular. At age eighteen: attractive appearance marred by repulsive yellow teeth; abandoned hopes of making basketball team after huffing and puffing his way from baseline to baseline; alienated from most social circles at school, as friends begin to resent Tim and the way he blatantly flaunts his cigarette use.

My grandmother—a repentant smoker. Her daily walks around our neighborhood are disrupted by fits of hacking coughs—chilling reminders of a deadly habit. Had my grandmother not faced her addiction early on in life, I might have already lost my closest relative and childhood role model.

As a young boy, my mother often warned me against smoking with pictures of cancerous lungs—lungs that looked more like charcoal briquettes than human organs. But the everyday examples, those of my uncle, my friend, and my grandmother, were the only warnings I needed growing up.

As a member of my school's speech and debate team, I work directly with underclassmen and supervise them on long-distance trips. Beyond teaching them how to excel in debate rounds, we help them realize the potential challenges they will face from the smoking population—those who have failed to realize tobacco's terrible side effects. As a role model and a leader on the team for these underclassmen, I have unfortunately seen a few kids lost to smoking, but I have also delighted in the fact that my support has prevented dozens of other debaters from falling into similar traps. I have influenced nearly every non-smoker on the team, and they, in turn, will provide smoke-free leadership for the future.

Colin Jost is a writer for *Saturday Night Live.*

The Eviction

Jacqueline Lalley

I submitted this essay to the editor of a humor column in a general inter-est magazine. He liked it and had a few suggestions, so I revised it for him, but in the end it was "too touching" for his venue. He suggested I submit it to the editor of another column at the same publication, with his rec-ommendation. Editor Two also liked it, but in order for it to fit with his column, there would have to be "more at stake for the narrator." To keep editing seemed like trying to fit my square peg into their round holes (hey, Editors One and Two—if you're into that, call me!), so I just decided to set it aside and accept their invitations to send them something else in the future. Later, I revised it again, and it was broadcast on public radio.

I am in my thirties and far too young to be a landlady. It seems like only yesterday my own landlord—a gnomish, bearded evangelist—was barging into my flat waving a club and accusing my roommate of being a witch. I was twenty. The word was "Wiccan."

Landlords were scum.

A couple of years ago, when I became one, I was determined to be different. No need to wave a club! How 'bout you mail the rent, I de-posit it into my nursing-home fund, and that's that? In fact, I was so out-of-your-face that I found a tenant on Craigslist and let her move in without meeting her or getting a credit report. I mean, why not? Donna worked a desk job for the U.S. Army Reserves—of course I could trust her. Plus, by renting to her, I was, you know, supporting our troops!

Things were great for about six months, but about halfway through her lease, Donna stopped paying rent. In my laissez-faire landlord haze, it took me a while to start asking the difficult questions, like: Where was my rent money? Why had she stopped paying? And, did I have to support our troops that much?

I knew I needed legal help, so I turned to my two friends from childhood who had actually done something with their lives. As it turns out, neither had experience in landlord/tenant law. One offered a rain check if my boss ever discriminated against me (I'm self-employed), and another vowed to defend me in a murder trial should things come to that. When I turned to the *Yellow Pages*, the young attorney at the other end of the line brightly listed all kinds of reasons Donna had a right to violate her lease, like that I hadn't given her a booklet about eating lead paint.

The lawyer I ended up hiring started out by informing me that I had a better chance of winning the Alabama state lottery than I did of collecting any money from Donna. (I looked it up; Alabama doesn't have a lottery.) Instead, I should focus on just getting her out of there.

Like most people, I had thought of eviction as a simple process where the sheriff comes and hauls the person's belongings to the curb, taking care to arrange the brassieres on top. But after receiving a bunch of notices and missing a bunch of court dates over the course of several months, Donna moved herself out. Still, I was hoping to find a little forensic evidence in the place to explain what had happened. Nothing big—a syringe here or automatic weapons cache there would have sufficed.

Instead, I found a few dust bunnies chasing stray hairbands and earrings across the bare hardwood floors. The guys from the sheriff's office, who had entered with their hands on their guns, gave me a look that said, "Call us when you've got actual sheriff's office business, will you?" and left.

I opened a kitchen drawer and found it stuffed with the kind of mundane ephemera that I sincerely hope will vanish along with my soul when I depart this earth, because all it takes is a quick survey of someone else's pizza coupons to realize that, aside from a few expiration dates, we're all the same.

But as I dug, I came across a few artifacts that began to unlock the mystery that was Donna.

There was the slip of paper, ostensibly a shopping list, which read simply:

- Air freshener
- Mesh panties
- Razor

Sounds like a lovely evening, I thought.

There was a business card from someone who sold jewelry and scarves and called herself The Accessorizer. Jesus, I thought, she can't make rent, but she's hired—not just *an* accessorizer, but *The* Accessorizer?!

There were no love letters or military secrets or—this would be cool—combinations of the two. The closest thing to personal correspondence was a few envelopes addressed to Donna by someone who could as easily have been a reviled aunt as a friend.

In the end, the answer came in the form of bills—dozens of bills, Urgent Statements, and letters from the lawyers of people whom Donna owed lots of money—people like me. There was a kitchen drawer full of them, and when I went to unlock the mailbox, it popped open like a really, really depressing jack-in-the-box.

Donna had been deep in debt even when she moved in. She must have borrowed some money to cover the first few months' rent and figured that after that, she'd ride the pre-eviction wave as long as she could.

After several hours and several trips to the Dumpster, I rested my hand on a doorknob and felt a thin chain draped across it. It was a medallion of Christopher, the patron saint of travelers. Having been de-canonized by the Roman Catholic Church, Christopher, too, was an evictee of sorts, only he didn't leave behind any coupons.

If Donna was like St. Christopher, then I was . . . God, did I really want to be the Roman Catholic Church in this scenario? Or any scenario, other than the one where I get to tell people it's okay to use birth control? I made up my mind then and there to always meet people before they move in—and get a credit report.

When I left, I took the medallion, dropped it into an envelope, and sent it off to someone I hope was Donna's friend. Maybe they could help return it to her. Maybe I'm not landlord scum. Not yet.

Jacqueline Lalley is a contributor to the *The Onion, Bitch Magazine,* and several anthologies. The list of magazines that have rejected her poetry does not include the *Harvard Review, Court Green,* or *Konundrum Engine Literary Review.*

Cartoon Limbo

Lewis Matheney

Between 1947 and 1949, an unknown cartoonist exchanged letters with a friend in which he lamented the business of pitching his cartoons to publishers and having them turned down. He conveyed his joy over signing a contract to do a syndicated strip, but then the disappointment of having that contract canceled before his work ever went to print. He doodled a rough sketch of a cartoon idea in one of the letters and concluded that cartoonists must "always have an iron in the fire." Two years later, in 1952, that cartoonist's strip, *Peanuts,* was picked up for syndication and it, along with that unknown cartoonist, Charles Schulz, became a defining part of popular culture and history.

The Schulz–*Peanuts* story exemplifies the experience that is universal among cartoonists as their work finds its way into, and sometimes out of, a sort of cartoon limbo.

For the accomplished cartoonist, the limbo experience is no big deal. It's just a part of some master plan. In this plan, limbo is karma; limbo is paying your dues. Do time in limbo and you'll see your way into the Promised Land at some point. Resist limbo and stay forever in limbo, it's that simple.

Such is the plight of the weak-hearted newcomer. Imagine the poor soul as he or she gleefully hands in a freshly hatched idea to an editor, only to have it immediately stapled to a standard issue rejection note and returned. Down comes the gloom and despair, freezing the hand and drying up the ink pen. For them, limbo is a dark, empty place in which their only happy return is a resounding echo when they call out, "Hello? Is anybody out there?"

It was fitting, therefore, that some of the legendary figures of cartoon and comic art would be the first to say yes to being a part of an exhibit I curated and hosted in New York City in January 2007 called *Cartoon Limbo.* They knew their place, firmly rooted alongside other legends who have all done time in limbo.

I invited around a thousand artists to join *Cartoon Limbo* and I found this to be true: the lesser known the artist (translation: the *younger* the artist), the more likely it was that they would say no. Responses from newbies ranged from hesitation and confusion to being downright indignant at the idea that they should be associated with—*gasp!*—rejected cartoonists.

The Charles Schulz Museum, in fact, was the first to say yes to *Limbo,* followed immediately by The Thurber House, Bunny Hoest and *The Lockhorns,* Mort Walker and *Beetle Bailey,* and *Archie* comic legend Stan Goldberg.

In all, twenty-nine artists and/or estates and museums representing cartoon and comic art, editorial cartoons, illustration in a cartoon style, and animation were exhibited in *Cartoon Limbo,* and their stories told a great deal about the outright rejection and nuanced slighting off that goes on in the life of a cartoonist.

For some, rejection comes in the form of a slap in the face. Take Gerry Greengrass, for example, whose work has ranged from self-penned and illustrated books (*Bow Wow Yoga,* Penguin, 2003, and *I Can Remember,* Tarcher/Putnam, 2001) to covers for books and record albums, as well as cartoons for *Playboy* in the 1960s. At some point, Gerry was invited to a party thrown by *Playboy.* Having done all of her correspondence by mail, she had not actually spoken to or met the cartoon editor in person. Gerry went to the party, asked around for the editor, and was finally pointed in his direction. She went over to him, shook his hand, and introduced herself. The editor's jaw dropped. "But you're a woman!" he declared, and from that point forward, she never sold another cartoon to, or had any response from, *Playboy* again. Clearly a case of 1960s chauvinism, but for Gerry Greengrass, it simply sealed her place in limbo with this particular institution forever.

Limbo isn't always self-inflicted, as could be the case of the newbie cartoonist who faints dead away after receiving his or her first severe punch to the gut. Cartoonist Ruth Marcus seems to have it all: limitless creative energy, fresh ideas, drive, and determination, not to mention a profound (but mostly overlooked) history as a successful cartoonist. Her *Small Wonders* cartoon feature ran for around ten years in *Good Housekeeping,* followed by three syndicated strips during the '60s and early '70s: *Oh, Lady! G. P. Jones,* and *Bi-Focals,* as well as her book *The Wife* (Price, Stearn, and Sloan, 1967, based on the strip *Oh, Lady!*). Marcus's vivid color in her current cartoons is a fresher-than-computer rendering almost entirely made up of hand-cut paper. A visit to her studio reveals boxes of the stuff she's amassed from a variety of sources: candy wrappers, gift wrapping, newspaper print, food packaging products, foil, tissue, and color copies of fabric. Her paper sources seem endless, the number of cartoons she has created through this intricate and detailed process number in the hundreds, and the number of punchlines and gags she is able to conjure up would lead you to believe she is a comedy historian, if not performer, utilizing everything from classic Vaudeville rim shots to something that sounds like the most current brand of stand-up comedy. Still, can she get a publisher for her broad-appeal book of cartoons about the joys and tribulations of new babies, motherhood, parenthood, and grandparenthood entitled *Bundles of Joy?* "Take my book, *please,*" is the battle cry for this unsung cartoonist who, along with her work, has been in limbo for years now.

As a children's book writer and illustrator, the words I have heard most often from editors are "sophisticated," "funky," and "cutting edge," always preceded by the word *too. Too* sophisticated, *too* funky, and *too* cutting edge for children, as if the editors actually sit and read to and draw for children as often as I do and have made a discovery

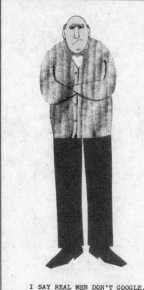

I SAY REAL MEN DON'T GOOGLE.

I LOVE THIS FAUX FUR JACKET BUT I HATE KNOWING
THAT SOME INNOCENT LITTLE FAUX DIED TO MAKE IT.

Detail of two-page spread of cut-paper cartoon art from book *Bundles of Joy* by Ruth Marcos.

for themselves that children are not sophisticated, funky, or cutting edge.

Undeterred, I started a small publishing company with my partner, published a book of my poetry and cartoons and am endlessly delighted at the sophistication, funkiness, and cutting-edge ideas that children bring with them when they come to see me read and draw at in-store events or at schools.

As curator and host of *Cartoon Limbo*, it was exhilarating to be in the company of the artist whose work redirected my drawing style in my early teenage years, extracting it from the entanglement of years of teaching by art teachers who had presumably good intentions but whose lessons had left me with a drawing style that was not my own. It was a sort of lifeless, "real" way of drawing that felt entirely foreign and looked derivative, deflated, and dull to me. The artist whose work

Illustration from *Zoom Cat Zoom!*

rescued me from all that is James Thurber. Upon seeing Thurber's en-
ergetic, hilarious, and often unfinished drawings for the first time
when I was around thirteen years old, I was able to free my hand up
and draw in a way that hadn't felt that real since maybe kindergarten.

I was giddy upon hearing the news that The Thurber House
would join *Cartoon Limbo*. Their contribution was the only non-
printed material included in the show—a video of a wonderful interview of Thurber by a very young Alistair Cooke. In it, Thurber relates
the story of having *The New Yorker* publisher Harold Ross being baffled
by an odd cartoon involving a barking seal, a cartoon Ross rejected
but later decided should be used. Upon returning to Thurber to ob-
tain the rejected piece, Ross discovered that Thurber had thrown it
away. Ross, of course, simply demanded that Thurber draw it again.
Bafflement also accompanied a decision regarding a cartoon of
Thurber's in which a man introduces to a party guest his present wife,
along with his former wife who is crouched atop a bookcase staring
down at the party. The seal cartoon and the former wife on the bookcase cartoon are signature cartoons of Thurber's, both of which
nearly met a permanent entombment in cartoon limbo.

Make no mistake, all the greats in cartooning have done time in
limbo. Even Dr. Seuss is no exception. A famous bit of rejection hap-

pened to Seuss at the very peak of his career. This was a career, however, that existed prior to his fame as a children's book writer and illustrator. Seuss was one of the more famous and successful cartoonists of his era, as seen mostly in his sharp political work and the hip advertising campaigns with which he was associated. Seuss was especially adept at aiming a glaring spotlight on human injustice through his political cartoons and his work often attacked crimes against Jews and African-Americans. He was able, therefore, to bring a high profile, respect of his peers, a history of being prolific, and an avid following by the general public to the table when he presented his idea for a children's book to publishers. However, editor after editor dismissed him and his work, sending back to limbo a manuscript and art that they deemed as too outlandish.

And to Think That I Saw It on Mulberry Street received approximately twenty-eight rejections before it was finally accepted by Random House in 1937.

The single political cartoon that appeared in *Cartoon Limbo* came from Jeff Danziger, who, upon reading the list of participating cartoonists I sent him, admonished me for not having more political cartoons in the exhibit. I was unable to come up with an explanation for this phenomenon, which I felt was in no way associated with my previous theory of young idealism and resistance to limbo. On the contrary, there were over a hundred political cartoonists whose careers had seen longevity, success, and multiple awards whom I had invited to be in the exhibit, but Danziger alone was the political cartoonist who said yes. Of the twenty-nine cartoonists in *Cartoon Limbo*, many offered multiple pieces to be shown in the exhibit. Danziger, however, offered one piece. The image is bold, in-your-face, and controversial—just what I felt a political cartoon should be. I enlarged it so that it would be one of the biggest pieces in the exhibit. Each of the cartoonists in *Limbo* were exhibited on four-foot-wide by eight-foot-high pieces of black foamcore. Danziger's cartoon, in some ways, faced off with the rest of the show—a somber, tough reminder of current politics in an exhibit of otherwise light-hearted

fare. It stood in the center of a wall that faced visitors from most any vantage point in the exhibit. In the end, this one piece whose final fate or destination in the publishing world I can't quite recall was far more effective than twenty or thirty other political pieces could have been.

In some form of therapy I experienced along the way—a guided meditation tape, I think it was—there's this fairly memorable lesson I got regarding how to deal with feelings. When an undesirable feeling like anxiety or anger arises, stop for a moment and *welcome* the feeling, maybe even *embrace* the feeling. Then simply ask yourself and the feeling why it's there. Dig deep and see what the lesson is that you're supposed to be getting from its presence. Tell the feeling it's free to go at any moment, but above all, do not put up resistance; it's the resistance that very often brings about bad health—which is much more than the bad feeling itself can do.

Sound preposterous? Wait till you find yourself in Cartoon Limbo. Just *try* putting up a fight and see what happens. I would say to you: Relax, kick back, and enjoy the ride. Remind yourself what great company you're in, if not in the present reality, then on some tran-

it's 2010! time for a LOOK BACK at RUDY's POST-MAYORAL DRAG CAREER

LET'S GO BACK TO 2002, THE YEAR RUDY TACKLED THE CABARET SCENE AS

GIULENA HORNE!

FANS OF JAZZ AND STANDARDS DID NOT TAKE WELL TO HIS INFUSION OF TIRELESS RAGE INTO NUMBERS LIKE "MISS OTIS REGRETS."

CRITICS CALLED HIS LENGTHY BETWEEN-SET MONOLOGUES, WHERE HE MOSTLY RAILED AGAINST PORN SHOPS, **"BAFFLING AND UNBEARABLE."**

NEXT, RUDY ACQUIRED THE RIGHTS TO "GILLIGAN'S ISLAND," RE-WRITING THE PERKY MARY ANN CHARACTER AS A DOMINEERING **GIULIANNE.**

VIEWERS FOUND IT PAINFUL TO WATCH RUDY FOR A FULL HALF-HOUR WEEKLY SCREAMING, **"I'M THE SKIPPER AROUND HERE NOW! YOU'LL DO AS I SAY!"**

HIS ONE-WOMAN SHOW
GIULENE DIETRICH: MY LEGENDARY SELF,

OPENED TO HALF-EMPTY HOUSES OF MOSTLY SUPPORTIVE FAMILY MEMBERS AND FRIENDS.

THEATRE-GOERS SENT A RESOUNDING "NO" TO A FLESH-REVEALING RUDY. CRITICS AGREED, IMPLORING RUDY IN A FULL-PAGE AD:

"HANG UP THE WIG ALREADY!"

Rejected cartoon pitched to *The New Yorker*'s Back Page feature by Lewis Matheney

scendental plane with all the legendary greats who have gone on before you. It's probably just a matter of time before you're released from limbo, and then what? You're hopefully a little wiser and maybe a little better prepared for it the next time it happens. Truth is, if you're any good as a cartoonist, it's going to happen next week, and next

Cover for *The New Yorker* by John Agee, rejected

week, and next month, and next year, and so on and so forth—probably for the rest of your life. Seriously—welcome to Cartoon Limbo.

Cartoon Limbo was exhibited at Venu Gallery, 417 Lafayette Street, in New York City's East Village from January 5 through February 2, 2007.

Featured artists were as follows: (in alphabetical order) Jon Agee, Santiago "Chago" Armada, Carl Barks, Dick Briefer, Art Cumings, Jeff Danziger, Simone Di Bagno, Stan Goldberg, Naxieli Gomez, Gerry Greengrass, Woody Guthrie, Irwin Hasen, Bunny Hoest, Crockett Johnson, Michael Klein, Karla Kuskin, Mike Lynch, Ruth Marcus, Lewis Matheney, John Reiner, Sergio Ruzzier, Charles Schulz, Maurice Sendak, Dr. Seuss, Monica Sheehan, Jay Stephens, James Thurber, Joe Vissichelli, and Mort Walker.

Lewis Matheney is the author and illustrator of *Zoom Cat Zoom!* (GLM Books) and illustrator of *Ice Cream Dreams* by Karla Kuskin. His cartoons and illustrations have been exhibited at the Chrysler Building, Cornelia Street Cafe, Paradisus 121, Venu Gallery, and Formerly Gaga in New York City. He is a member of the Society of Children's Book Writers and Illustrators and the Poetry Society of America. He was named one of the Top 100 Cool New Yorkers by the *Daily News* and resides in New York City, Chicago, and Stockton, New Jersey.

Acknowledgments

Thank you to my terrific editors, Julia Cheiffetz and Jillian Quint, for always having my back, for their enthusiasm about this book, and for putting their faith in my instincts. Thanks to everyone at Ballantine Books for truly allowing this book to happen.

Thank you to Kate Lee for her patience and for taking so much time to work with me and teach me how to get this started and to keep it going. Thanks to everyone at ICM for their support and enthusiasm.

Thanks to my brother, Andy, for leading by example and for always looking out for my best interest. Thanks to Millie, Sammy, Fred, Fay, Marcia, Kenny, Justin, Melissa, Linda, John, Debbie, Paul, Tara, Maeve, Walker, and Orin for making Thanksgiving fun (you all do more than that "and you know it").

Thanks to Schack Realty for allowing me to operate their freight elevator while I worked on the proposal for this book.

Thanks to Laura Newmark for all of her hard work and to Kris O'Hagan, Michael Mallamo, Andrew Herbert West, Kim Cavallaro, Bobby Henderson, Lang Fisher, Emily Sachs, Joanne and Nichole Somma, Rachel Kramer Bussel, Wendy Spero, Todd Rosenberg, Jeff Lesh, Bababooey, Peter and Kim Kassnove, and Chris Genoa and Sara Schaefer.

Thanks to Adam Cole-Kelly, Matt Diffee, Jon Bulette, and The Defibulators for their hard work for *The Rejection Show*. Thanks to Justin

Krebs and The Tank, Performance Space 122, Mo Pitkin's House of Satisfaction, Anthony King, Pat Baer and The Upright Citizen's Brigade Theater, everyone at Comix NYC, and Rififi for allowing me to do my thing.

Thanks to anyone and everyone who has written about and helped spread the word about The Rejection Show, including NPR and WNYC, ABC News, Los Angeles Times, Newsday, The New Yorker magazine, New York Daily News, The Onion, the blogosphere, and everyone else who has taken an interest.

Of course, thank you to the contributors of this book and, perhaps more important, everyone that was rejected from this book. See you guys on The Rejection Show.

Finally, to all of the past and future Rejection Show performers and to all of my peers in the New York City comedy scene—I have never felt so welcomed and supported by a group of people in my life. Without you I would not have had the opportunity to work on any of the projects that I will be working on today, tomorrow, and in the future. I love you all.

JON FRIEDMAN is an award-winning comedian and a writer and producer from New York City. He is the creator and host of the critically acclaimed *The Rejection Show* as well as the New York City Beard & Moustache Championships, The Delicious Sandwich Social, and many other popular live events. He recently launched and edits *rejectionshow.com,* known to the world as "the Web's official home for all things rejected." Jon and his works have been featured in the *Los Angeles Times,* on NPR, *ABC News,* and many more media outlets. He has performed and read at literary events and stand-up comedy venues throughout New York City and beyond.